Raising
Grandkids

*University of Regina Press designates one title
each year that best exemplifies the guiding
editorial and manuscript production principles
of long-time senior editor Donna Grant.*

Raising Grandkids

Inside Skipped-Generation Families

GARY GARRISON

 University of Regina Press

Printed and bound in Canada by Marquis. The text of this book is printed on 100% post-consumer recycled paper with earth-friendly vegetable-based inks.

Cover design: Duncan Campbell, University of Regina Press
Text design: John van der Woude, JVDW Designs
Copy editor: Ryan Perks
Proofreader: Kristine Douaud
Cover art: "Holding Hands" by Darrya/iStockphoto.

Library and Archives Canada Cataloguing in Publication

Garrison, Gary, 1948-, author
    Raising grandkids : inside skip-generation families / Gary Garrison.

Issued in print and electronic formats. ISBN 978-0-88977-554-1 (softcover).—ISBN 978-0-88977-555-8 (PDF).—ISBN 978-0-88977-556-5 (HTML)

1. Grandparents as parents. 2. Grandparenting. 3. Grandparent and child. 4. Grandchildren—Care. 5. Parenting. I. Title.

HQ759.9.G375 2018   306.874'5   C2018-903211-1   C2018-903212-X

10 9 8 7 6 5 4 3 2

University of Regina Press, University of Regina
Regina, Saskatchewan, Canada, S4S 0A2
tel: (306) 585-4758 fax: (306) 585-4699
web: www.uofrpress.ca

We acknowledge the support of the Canada Council for the Arts for our publishing program. We acknowledge the financial support of the Government of Canada. / Nous reconnaissons l'appui financier du gouvernement du Canada. This publication was made possible with support from Creative Saskatchewan's Creative Industries Production Grant Program.

*To grandparents everywhere who raise grandchildren,
and to everyone who shares themselves with younger
generations to make a better future for everyone.*

Relationships are the agents of change and the most powerful therapy is human love.
—*Dr. Bruce Perry,* The Boy Who Was Raised as a Dog

Contents

Acknowledgements

I'd like first to thank my partner Sara, whose love and kindness have inspired and revitalized me. I'm grateful for the parenting I received from my parents, Donald and Amelia Garrison, and I'm grateful for their parents as well, Pearl and Joseph Schott and Mose and Doolah Garrison.

For their support of my work on this book and for their work with grandparents and other caregivers, I thank Betty Cornelius and the entire CANGRANDS circle, Drs. Andrew Bremness and Wanda Polzin and the other staff of CASA Edmonton, grandparent support groups across the country, caseworkers in the child welfare system, the supervisors and politicians and journalists who are working to make the system better, and all the grandparents who are doing their best in difficult circumstances and the extended families who work with them.

I'd like especially to thank everyone who agreed to be interviewed for this book, regardless of whether their contributions are reproduced below. I am grateful to the Alberta Foundation for the Arts and the Edmonton Arts

Council for financial support, and to the Banff Centre for a magnificent and inspiring space to write.

Though he's not quoted in the book, my neighbour, Jonathan Hooton's conversations with me about his work in intergenerational and childhood trauma significantly broadened my knowledge of the subject and increased my confidence in writing about it.

I am grateful to Bruce Walsh of the University of Regina Press for his confidence in me, as well as to others at the URP, including Sean Prpick, David McClellan, Ryan Perks, Donna Grant, and Kelly Laycock, all of whom helped see this project through to completion.

Author's Note

In the last thirty years, laws governing privacy and access to government information have not kept up with the social changes wrought by Facebook, Twitter, Instagram, and people's ability to access data that moves at the speed of light. Some say the Earth is racing toward a catastrophe of massive coastal flooding, species extinction, and human self-destruction. Others claim the planet will heal herself and that our species will evolve to a place previous cultures reserved for angels and gods. There's some truth in both viewpoints. It's also true that this brave new world has destroyed people like Rehtaeh Parsons, the Nova Scotia 15-year-old driven to suicide by cyberbullies. For good reason, it's illegal to publicize the names of children without the consent of their caregivers, and there are good reasons for those caregivers to withhold consent.

I am committed to protecting the identities of the grandparents, parents, and children to whose lives I have had the honour to bear witness in these pages. In sharing their personal stories with me, they trusted me with their most precious possessions, and I have done my best to keep them safe.

The grandparents in this book have all been gagged to some degree. They know that if they told their stories publicly—on the evening news, say, or on the Internet—they would risk losing whatever government support they have. Indeed, the state could apprehend the very grandchildren they are sacrificing their lives to protect. Many are also afraid of further alienating their own sons and daughters, the parents of the grandchildren they are raising. And yet they are eager to speak up. They want to tell all grandparents who raise grandchildren that they are not alone, that they have no reason to be ashamed of the fact that their own children cannot or will not raise the babies they brought into the world. They want others to learn from their experiences of standing up for themselves against an impersonal, bullying system. They want to tell everyone, as I try in this book, that they are their neighbours and that they are proud of what they do, of the challenges, suffering, joys, sacrifices, and successes they experience in this retirement activity called "grandparenting."

For these reasons I have chosen pseudonyms for the grandparents and grandchildren in this book unless they have insisted on putting their names out in public. Their identities are as sacred as their stories. But while their stories are for readers to witness, participate in, and see themselves in, their identities are for themselves alone.

Foreword

In my previous book, *Human on the Inside*, I talked about the nature of systems, how human beings need systems to frame how we live and interact and how at the same time these systems dehumanize us, turning us into mere customers, clients, inmates, files, bar codes, or pixels on a screen. In that book, my focus was the prison system in Canada, but all systems—whether it's marriage, religion, criminal justice, income tax, education, health care, you name it—embody the same principle. For us to be safe and healthy, whether as a community or as individuals, we need to find a balance between connecting with each other as persons and relying on systems that treat us as objects.

This person-object tension is central to the life of everyone who cares for children who have to live separate from their parents, and, of course, to the lives of the children themselves. When a baby is born to an abusive mother or an addicted or runaway father—to pick one example—who cares for the baby? The law says that if I know a child is being abused, I'm obligated to report it. But if I'm the grandparent, and reporting the abuse means a child welfare caseworker gets involved, I'm turning my own granddaughter over to a system that wears a human face but is essentially a bureaucratic-political machine. Like the Tin Man in *Wizard of Oz* before he gets a heart, the system doesn't have the capacity to love her. But the Tin Man is cute and lovable compared to the system I'm talking about. The impersonal malevolence of Hal the computer in *2001: A Space Odyssey* or the Borg in *Star Trek: The Next Generation* is more like it. The child welfare system employs people who want to help but is designed more to avoid public scandal at minimal cost than to do what is best for the child and her family.

I have great admiration and sympathy for child welfare workers who take responsibility for society's most traumatized children and want to help horribly dysfunctional families. But as a grandparent-caregiver, I cannot trust a caseworker any more than I can a "friend" of a "friend" on Facebook. I have to develop a support network that functions like my own brain, one that builds neural pathways that work for me and prunes away those I don't use or want. I have to find friends and family members who will support me, my partner, and our grandchildren, who will share experiences with us, commiserate with us, and suggest options we didn't know about.

My support network necessarily has The Government as a backstop. That's how society works. But the government has no more ability to solve personal problems than a hundred dollar bill has to heal a child's post-traumatic stress. The money can buy food for the child, but only other people connecting with the child at a personal level can help heal her wounds.

When grandparents are the closest people to the child, they face unique challenges having to do with their relationships to the child's missing parents, their own health, their fixed incomes, their energy levels, et cetera. They also have unique advantages: the wisdom of lived experience, the family connection to the child, the love for the child they've had since she was born.

It takes a village to raise a child who has a healthy relationship with her parents. It takes a wide network of loving people to raise a traumatized child. That network includes medical doctors, psychologists, and psychiatrists skilled in applying the latest discoveries in brain research and the impact of addictions. When grandparents are the primary caregivers, they can offer the child a unique personal touch, but their family, friends, and neighbours must honour and love the grandparents for what they do and who they are if they are to succeed their second time around as parents.

Grandparents into the Breach

We are involved in creating the
future for humankind.

—*Dr. Bruce Perry*[1]

A slim, fair-haired girl in a pink sundress asks 7-year-old Jack, "Where do you go to school?" Jack and I are waiting in the checkout line at a Safeway in central Edmonton; the girl, accompanied by a woman about my age—in her sixties I'd say—is behind us. Jack blushes through his olive-brown cheeks and turns toward the display of candy bars and magazines. He's naturally shy, even more so around girls his age.

I turn to the woman, who's leaning on the handle of a grocery cart full of produce and pasta. "Do you live around here?" I ask. She glances at my bald crown, the curly grey hair jutting out around the temples of my

---

1 This epigraph comes from my notes on Dr. Bruce Perry's presentation at the Caregiver Training Conference in Edmonton, Alberta, on April 13, 2014.

wire-framed glasses, a faded purple Edmonton Folk Fest T-shirt from five years ago on my chest. She gives me a blank look. Maybe she wonders how to demonstrate to the girl that she should not talk to strange men. And I admit that I do look a little strange to some people, and sometimes, when I look in the bathroom mirror in the morning, even to myself.

"I'm Gary," I say. "This is my grandson, Jack. He's going into grade 2 at Grandin School in August." I nod toward the girl. "What school does she go to?"

When I say "grandson," the woman's eyes glisten. Maybe she thinks I'm not so strange after all. Or perhaps she realizes we're both the same kind of strange. She tells me that they're not from the neighbourhood, but they live not far away. She says she and her 8-year-old granddaughter live together. She tells me the name of her child's school. As the checkout clerk takes my twenty dollar bill, I say goodbye to the woman and the girl. They smile.

It's been thirty years since my own kids were cute enough to break the ice with strangers at grocery stores, parks, or shopping centres. But now that I'm grandfathering two small children, this happens every day, everywhere I go. I've met grandparents with grandchildren in restaurants and on sidewalks. Reading my poems about grandparenting in public, I've had grandparents come up to me afterwards and say, "Me too!" Friends have told me about grandparents they know in situations like mine and offer to introduce me to them.

Grandparents are everywhere. That's where we belong. But the grandparenting some of us do is the other side of the moon compared to the grandparenting we got when we were kids during the 1950s and '60s. For us, a visit to grandma and grandpa was a treat if they lived nearby and a vacation trip to paradise if they didn't. Grandma and grandpa didn't make us do stuff we didn't want to, like eat broccoli or wash dishes. They didn't discipline us or threaten to spank us when we did something bad. They played with us in the park. They bought us candy. They gave us toys and money, even when it wasn't Christmas or a birthday. Most grandparents our age do grandparenting like that now. It's an occasional, part-time break from retirement.

But the grandparenting I'm talking about is full-time mothering and fathering young children who would've ended up in foster care if we didn't take them in. We raise the children as our own, but we raise them with thirty more years of life experience than when we raised children the first time. We raise them because somebody saw these kids being neglected or abused and phoned child welfare. We raise them because we saw parenting that had gone horribly wrong and we wanted to keep child welfare out of it. We raise them because their biological parents—our children—can't or won't, whether because of addiction, mental or physical illness, death, imprisonment, poverty, or marriage breakup.

We raise them while we nurse a wound deep in our hearts, because our child is out of the picture, because we fear for our child's safety, because when the telephone rings we shudder: maybe this time it's the police and they've found our son or daughter dead from a self-inflicted wound or drug overdose. We raise these grandchildren even though we're chronically sleep deprived. We wrestle every night with the voice inside our head that says, "Mike could be out in the snowstorm tonight, freezing to death." We imagine Amanda prostituting herself for crystal meth or Mitchell burglarizing a pharmacy.

We walk or bus or drive these grandkids to school every day. We take them to soccer, hockey, music, dance, tae kwon do. We have more in common with the grandparents we sit next to at these events than with the parents, but we don't belong to either group. We can't socialize with retired friends because we have kids to parent every school day after 3:00 p.m., all day on weekends, on PD days, school holidays, and all summer. We get emergency calls from the school office, as parents do, and have to interrupt our days for our grandkids' dental and medical appointments. But we're thirty years older than the other parents. We grew up on the Beatles, the Rolling Stones, the Who—not Pearl Jam, the Stone Temple Pilots, or Brittney Spears. We learned to read in phonics class, watched snowy black-and-white television images via rooftop antennae, and dialed clunky landline telephones to talk to friends on party lines. These cultural influences shaped our brains a long time ago, and those brains don't work as fast now as when we were parents the first time.

We raise these grandkids because they're ours; they're members of our family, and we love them. Despite the anxiety, fear, shame, guilt, expense, loss of freedom, and frustrated dreams of retirement, we still love them.

The manager of Kinship Care in Alberta told me that 1,400 kinship families in the province get government support of some kind. About 90 per cent of these caregivers are grandparents. Betty Cornelius, president and founder of CANGRANDS National Kinship Support, told me Ontario officially has 22,000 kincare[2] families. But nobody knows how many grandparents are raising grandchildren informally, without government involvement. At the first kincare Christmas party I went to in Edmonton, I met a grandfather who claimed a million Canadian grandparents were raising grandchildren. The real story, though, isn't statistics. It's the individual grandparents and grandchildren who live together as a family unit, with all the struggle and delight that involves.

Extended family members have cared for children for millennia. Our hunter-gatherer ancestors who lived in caves or lean-tos stuck together in extended family and tribal groups against the threat of wolves, bears, and saber-toothed tigers. Sharing responsibility for the tribe's children was as natural as sharing food and fire. Today, it's normal in places like China for grandparents

---

2   "Kincare" is the generic term used to refer to Kinship Care, a government program that supports extended family members who raise a child for a relative(s) who either can't or won't. Kincare also includes coaches, teachers, or family friends who agree to raise a child as their own.

to raise children when the mother and father both have to work. The HIV/AIDS epidemic in Africa has challenged grandmothers more than ever to step up and raise untold millions of orphans.[3] Kinship caregiving is a common cultural practice in Indigenous communities throughout the world, and it's an honourable thing to do. But mainstream Western culture has attached a stigma to it: if a grandmother is raising a grandchild, the thinking goes, she must have failed as a parent—and here she is, doing it again! It's part of our tradition of devaluing women of every age and undervaluing elders too. In North America, systemic anti-Indigenous racism has for centuries included devaluing all aspects of Indigenous culture. In Canada, we still grapple with the intergenerational trauma of the residential school system, the racist, genocidal logic of which extended to the so-called '60s Scoop, and which lives on in the disproportionate numbers of Indigenous children in our child welfare systems today.

Developmental psychologist John Bowlby, author of a seminal book on broken childhood, says the practice, so prevalent in Western industrialized nations, of parents migrating for employment places severe pressure on those parents to go it alone, without a village of relatives to support them. He says, "In any analysis of the causes of children becoming deprived, therefore, it has to be considered not

---

3 The Stephen Lewis Foundation has been publicizing and supporting these grandmothers since 2003. What happened to the grandfathers who could be helping them? They may be far away working to support the family—a long tradition in Africa—or they may have died or simply left.

only why the natural home group has failed, but also why relatives have failed to act as substitutes."[4] In the last twenty years, Western governments have offered varying degrees of financial support, encouragement, and training to extended family caregivers and even to teachers, coaches, and neighbours with whom the child has had a previous relationship.

Grandparents are by far the largest of these kinship groups. And yet many grandparents keep secret the fact that they are raising grandchildren. Some realize they need to be with others like themselves in order to feel normal again, to share experiences, and to cope with an ever-shifting torrent of difficulties. In the summer of 2012, I met thirty grandparents and seventy grandchildren at Camp Ignite, located in southern Ontario on the shore of Roblin Lake, next to historic Ameliasburgh. These grandparents gathered for the CANGRANDS summer camp to support each other, shed tears, and celebrate together.

While children splashed in the pool, played volleyball, shot baskets, and dug in sandboxes, I interviewed ten grandparents in the camp's open areas, under the shade of 100-year-old ash trees. Occasionally the children interrupted to ask grandma or grandpa a question or to get a kiss for an owie. Sometimes grandma or grandpa yelled across the field for a child to behave. Even in this idyllic summer setting, none of us had the luxury of peace, quiet, and solitude; this was not a Caribbean resort or a seniors' recreation centre.

---

4   John Bowlby, *Child Care and the Growth of Love* (Harmondsworth, UK: Penguin, 1965), 85.

I got to know many of my peers at Camp Ignite, other grandparents who raise grandchildren, who help them heal profound psychological and physical wounds and thereby make a better future for these children, their families, and the world. This book celebrates and honours them for taking on this strenuous work at a time in their lives when their bodies tell them to slow down and society says they are past their prime. These grandparents are heroes. At great risk to themselves, they go into battle with social workers, judges, lawyers, and even their own sons and daughters to protect and nurture vulnerable grandchildren. Here are snapshots of a few of them.

Victoria is 74 years old and lives in St. Catharines, Ontario. She's raised her great-granddaughter for the last ten years, and now she also cares for her recently retired husband, who has Alzheimer's. On October 8, 2002, she took in her granddaughter's 5-day-old baby, who was born an alcoholic and now has serious brain damage due to fetal alcohol spectrum disorder, or FASD. Chapter 1 tells Victoria's story.

Lucy lives in Montreal with two granddaughters, 12 and 14. She's had them since they were born, when she was 50 years old. Her son, her only child, is their father. He's addicted to drugs and alcohol. He drops by to visit once a year and then promptly disappears again. The mother has been addicted to heroin since she was 17, and Lucy is surprised whenever she hears the mother is still alive. Every year when the parents' birthdays come around, Lucy and the girls sing happy birthday to the pictures of them that hang on the wall. The girls ask her, "Do you think we'll ever see mom before she dies?"

Don jokes about his ongoing battle with pancreatitis. "I should've died thirty years ago!" he says. When he has the energy, his inner schoolteacher surfaces. He commands the attention of over a hundred people in Camp Ignite's large cafeteria, his booming voice loud enough to drown out clinking cutlery and giggling children. But he has to take naps and medication every day to keep going. He and his wife, Cassie, care for an 8-year-old granddaughter full-time. The girl's mother has bipolar disorder and used to be heavily into ecstasy. Cassie and Don are retired teachers who spent $20,000 in a custody battle with the mother; they doubt that Caribbean cruises will be in their future, but they say they're so happy living with their grandchild that a mere cruise would be a step down for them.

Julie's stepdaughter was 27 when she got pregnant. For the first year, the baby was back and forth between her parents' home and Julie's. Julie said the parents were addicts who frequently beat each other up and trashed their home in the process. Julie and her husband spent a fortune battling the birth parents' legal aid lawyers to get custody. The stepdaughter brags about her daughter on her Facebook page and likes to be called mommy. When the stepdaughter comes for a rare visit, she gives her child a doll. Julie says that's the extent of her interest in mothering.

Chris lives in a mid-sized Ontario city with his extended Indigenous family. He jokes that he and his wife have taken in more than a hundred kids over the years. He says they have fourteen or more people sleeping over at their house some nights—so many that he sometimes has to sleep on the floor. He and his wife recently adopted seven-year-old twins who were daughters of his wife's cousin. "Now they're my daughters," he laughs, "but realistically, I think we count them as third cousins." He was in his early fifties when Children's Services told him he was too old to take the girls in; he and his wife convinced them to change their minds. Now Chris and his wife are educating themselves about FASD. They got the twins diagnosed, but now he needs to develop strategies to work with them. He's determined to educate his community about the long-term effects of drinking during pregnancy. Chapter 7 tells Chris's story.

Betty Cornelius, the president and founder of CAN-GRANDS, tells me that 95 per cent of the kids associated with CANGRANDS have FASD, ADHD, ODD, or some other disability.[5] She laughs, "And the other 5 per cent of the grandparents are delusional and think their kids don't have any of these things!" Once the children are diagnosed, grandparents can get financial help and other support. Getting that diagnosis, though, can be as tough as climbing a cliff with a child on your back, and it costs thousands of dollars. But governments are tight-fisted and often withhold information about programs for which grandchildren might be eligible. Chapter 13 tells Betty's story.

---

5   ADHD: attention deficit hyperactive disorder; ODD: oppositional defiant disorder.

At the CANGRANDS camp, a normal family group is one grandmother and up to five grandkids. Four grandfathers are there with partners, and one or two more drop in and out during the five-day event. At the end of the week, Betty Cornelius asks each of the grandparents to express a wish for the group. My wish is that more grandfathers get involved in the children's lives. My other wish is that grandparents in hiding will set their shame aside and take pride in the love they give their grandchildren every day.

But before we go any further, I have a confession to make. At the outset, I said Jack is my grandson, but he's technically a step-grandson: he and his sister are my partner's grandchildren. I've had a relationship with them both for nearly as long as I've had a relationship with their grandmother. But the more I get into the culture of kincare, foster care, adoption, traumatic attachment groups and the like, the more I realize the labels we use to identify our roles are inadequate, at best. I have three grandchildren by my own three biological children. I am functionally the father of the two I'm raising, but they have a hard time calling me dad, even when they give me cards on Father's Day. If I were their dad, would that make them brother and sister to my own three children? If so, that would make them the aunt and uncle to my biological grandchildren. If we adopted them, would that make them brother and sister to their own biological father? We tell the kids they have two sets of parents: the ones they were born to and us. For us, the important thing is our relationship with these children now, not who conceived them.

A few years ago, a friend I went to high school with in the 1960s and hadn't talked with much for thirty years asked me why I decided to help raise two grandkids that weren't mine. I said, "I've got nothing better to do." What could be better than living with the woman I love and helping her raise two grandchildren? If I'd found a woman to love who had no grandchildren in the house, of course, that would have been good too. But I didn't. In fact, the woman I love didn't have any grandchildren when our relationship started; she acquired them a little later. When I saw how much she loved them and what she was giving up to take them in, I loved her even more.

If I'd had the chance to be 35 years old again instead of 65, I might have taken it. That wasn't one of the options. But being around a 6-year-old girl and an 8-year-old boy is a good way to get back some of the youthful exuberance that my body had forgotten. Being in love helps me feel young again too. That it involves loving two kids and coaching them as they learn to read, write, skate, play soccer and hockey, ride bicycles, play violin, and dance, is a bonus, way better than getting anything at a three-for-one sale.

In the 1950s, when I was their age, I saw television ads that plugged Geritol, an iron supplement for older people. They claimed older people had low energy because of "tired blood," and Geritol would fix it. I'm in my middle sixties, and my blood often feels tired. So do my brain, my muscles, my eyes and ears. That all changes when I engage with a child many decades younger. Since I'm raising two of them, I get regular doses of something more effective than Geritol countless times every day. Of course, my blood does get plenty tired every evening when the kids are in bed and their grandmother and I finally have some free time.

Households like ours—headed by the grandparents with grandchildren present and the middle generation missing—are commonly called "skipped-generation families."[6] The numbers of such households is growing. People may think that our family setup is a little strange, but when I'm out with my partner and our two grandkids, it's clear that we are part of the new normal in parenting. And indeed, we are a living reminder of extended family units that have been around since our ancestors started walking upright and developed opposable thumbs.

None of us is a skipped-generation grandparent because we consciously decided our grandchildren were essential to the survival of the species. We took on the job out of love for them. My first encounter with a group of grandparents raising grandchildren was the CANGRANDS campout in 2012. Nobody there had to tell me they were doing it for love; their actions shouted it loud and clear.

---

6   Statistics Canada uses the term "skip-generation families." More recently, the term "grandfamilies" has also become common in the published literature.

ONE

The CANGRANDS Campout: A Great-Grandmother's Love Leaps Three Generation Gaps

Sit down, young lady. Don't you stand up here and lie to me. If that child did not get [FASD] from you, I'm damn well sure she didn't get it from great-grandma, because she didn't carry her! You did!
                                        —*Judge in family court*

On July 8, 2012, I drove into Ameliasburg, Ontario, turned right at the sign that identified Camp Ignite, and parked on the grass beside several other cars. It was a beautiful sunny day: bright blue sky, fluffy cumulus clouds drifting lazily from west to east, the temperature in the upper twenties, humidity in the seventies at least. Grandparents were gathered here to support each other like the fire ants that, by the thousands, linked their legs together and made living rafts so they could survive the flooding in Texas during Hurricane Harvey in 2017.

I walked into the main building to register and got a bear hug from Betty Cornelius, the founder and president of CANGRANDS. I'd talked to her on the phone about the camp. She'd encouraged me to come with the whole family, but that was impossible. She was delighted I'd come to represent Alberta, but I couldn't claim to speak for anyone else. Technically, she could claim, I represented everyone west of Sudbury, Ontario, and that a grandmother from Montreal represented everyone east of the Ottawa River. This twelfth annual CANGRANDS camp was primarily a southern Ontario event.

Approximately 100 campers were there: about 70 kids, 26 grandmothers, and 4 grandfathers—this out of the 280 or so grandparents Betty had on her CANGRANDS email list at the time, out of the 25 to 30 local chapters she'd started across the country. Canada's 2011 census tallied 72,665 skipped-generation grandparents, each of whom would've fit right in at the camp. Thousands were too busy raising grandchildren to come. Or they were working and couldn't spare the time, or were living on pensions and couldn't afford it. Betty told me the census number is way too low: many skipped-generation grandparents are too afraid, too ashamed, or simply too worn out to identify themselves with this group, even on a census form.

After Betty's greeting, I chatted with Dominic, whose wife, Amy, was handling the releases, cheques, and registration forms. I checked into my room: a bedroom big enough for eight or ten people in bunk beds, but I had it to myself. It was in a 1960s-vintage clapboard bunkhouse with tiny windows and a layer of dust thick as grey flannel on the windowsills and furniture. Experienced campers knew to bring electric fans, but nobody told me. It was just as well. A fan would have merely stirred up hot, humid air and dust. The daytime temperature was near thirty, and because of the high humidity it only dropped a few degrees overnight. My sinuses ran and my eyes burned day and night because of all that dust, and I was constantly blowing my nose. One grandmother took pity on me and gave me some antihistamine tablets. Without those magic pills, which I took twice a day, my stay would have been one long, sleepless sinus attack.

A film crew from TVOntario was on site, conducting interviews and taking shots of grandparents and kids at play. I walked around the grassy area beside the pool, the swings, the dorm rooms, and then on to the lakeshore. I introduced myself to people and chatted. Kids aged 2 to 16 ran around, tossed and kicked balls, splashed in the pool, dug in the sand, and waded into the lake. This could have been any school playground anywhere in the country. Well-behaved kids. Few visible disabilities. Every now and then a shrieking fit or an argument that a grandparent quickly shut down. Except for the handful of teenaged volunteers, none of the supervisors looked younger than about 55.

At the lakeshore, waiting for the dinner bell, I talked to a retired fire chief and his wife. Eight kids, all preteens, played in the water. Nobody was supervising them but us, and nobody had asked us to. We were simply part of the temporary village that cared for them. The ex–fire chief and his wife told me they'd been coming to the camp for a few years, like many others. They shared the details of their skipped-generation family with me as if I were a trusted uncle. In fact, everybody seemed to share intimate details of their family struggles with everybody else. They trusted Betty Cornelius to screen out risky strangers. Betty told me later that in over fifteen years of running CAN-GRANDS, she's only had one problem: a child's biological mother had posed as a grandmother online to find out what her own mother was saying about her.

After dinner, I sat at a picnic table under a huge ash tree, beside a grandmother who was eager for adult conversation, even with a stranger. She told me of her heart problems, that she'd planned to retire but went back to work in her mid-sixties so she could help support her daughter's five kids. She and her daughter shared custody. All five children were at the camp. Every now and then, she'd glance across the open area where the kids played and yell, "Smarten up, Jesse!" or, "Get out of that sandbox, Julie!"

She said all her kids had ADHD or FASD or prenatal brain damage caused by their mother's drug addiction. Her daughter was pregnant again, she said, and soon she'd be looking after six grandkids. She told me that what these kids need more than anything is love. Her own health and finances apparently didn't matter. She would love them all even if it killed her. When it was time for her to get the kids to bed, I wished her a good night's sleep. She looked at me with a forced smile and said, "Oh, does that mean you're going to look after my grandkids while I sleep?" Most of the kids at camp slept in groups with a teenager supervising them, but some of hers refused to spend the night with anyone but grandma. I watched her drag herself over to a child who had just come down the slide, and I wondered, "How long has it been since you had one good night's sleep?"

As another grandmother told me, "pretty well every one of the kids here has some kind of mental or neuro-logical problem." She said many of the people here send their kids to Camp Winston[1] every year for a week. That's even better than this camp, she said, because grandparents can drop the kids off and have one week of real retirement.

This grandmother told me that getting an FASD diag-nosis in Toronto was easy, but others at the camp said they knew people who moved from Ontario to Alberta to get diagnosed because Alberta is the best place in Canada for FASD support. I wondered about that, because I knew that the primary diagnostic clinic in Edmonton, the Glenrose Hospital, had a two-year waiting list, and even getting on it was difficult. I was new to this skip-generation gig, so I asked, What good is a diagnosis? Is

---

1 According to the Camp Winston website, "Camp Winston provides inspiring recreational opportunities for kids with complex neurological disorders who need highly specialized support." These disorders include autism, attention deficit hyperactivity, Tourette's, learning disabilities, obsessive compulsive disorder, and oppositional defiant disorder.

it more than a label? She said, "For one thing, they get a dog!" At a previous camp, she said, an FASD kid "viciously hammered" one of her kids with a basketball. She said he later got a big black service dog to help him keep calm, and that made a big difference. Then she laughed, "But the grandmother spends more time with the dog than the kid does!"

At Camp Ignite I participated in workshops, activities, and discussions. I talked shop with grandparents and kids in the cafeteria while we ate. When I described my book project to the group, almost everybody wanted me to interview them. They wanted everybody to know about skipped-generation families.

The most enthusiastic and outspoken was Victoria. She'd raised her great-granddaughter, Judy, since she was five days old. Victoria was lively, energetic, self-assured, and spoke with a melodious Newfoundland accent. In group discussions, she always had her hand up to speak. When we found a shady spot under a maple tree where we could sit across a picnic table from each other in relative quiet, I asked, "How old is your great-granddaughter?"

"Oh!" she said. "I'm tellin' ya! She'll be ten the third of October, and I'll have her ten years the eighth of October. It's been rough. But we survived." She's 74, but her voice and her eyes, the smile on her face, all sparkle with energy and optimism.

I said, "It sounds like you've done better than survive."

"Some people tell me that," she said. "But—" She paused and took a deep breath to hold a tear in check and steady her voice. "One day at a time. Definitely. It was really rough those first five years."

That's how long she fought her daughter and granddaughter for custody. "Legal battles with her mother. Went to Children's Aid six months. Then they asked the court to withdraw the case altogether, pending me getting custody. Took me five years and $40,000 lawyers' fees and court costs.

"Children's Aid was co-operative with me up to six months," she said. She gritted her teeth. Her voice turned cold and hard. "First they don't want me to have her. I was 'too old' to have her. I fought that out with them that day in court. Then they wanted the court to give them three weeks to investigate me. So the judge asks me if I had anything to say. So I gave them my whole life story. Then the judge said to the Children's Aid people, 'Now, what've you got to say to that?' 'Well, we understand she's recently got married.' The judge looked at me and said, 'You want to answer that?' I said, 'Twenty-five years! How recent would you call that?'

"Then the judge looked at them and at their lawyer and said, 'You call that recently married?' So the judge says to me, 'Don't you worry. That child is going home with you today.'"

Children's Aid insisted that they supervise the arrangement, and the judge asked Victoria what she thought of that. She answered, "I'll tell you the same thing I told the Children's Aid worker at the hospital on Saturday: They can come. They can park their behind on my chesterfield or chair 24/7 so long as they don't interfere with my work. So the judge said, 'Well, she's being co-operative. Now you better be co-operative with her, because I'm telling you, don't you go without giving her twenty-four hours' notice.'"

But the judge wasn't too happy about Victoria's intention to take in the child's mother too. Victoria said she wanted to give the mother, Natalie, a chance to prove herself, to learn to care for Judy. Victoria said she'd teach her. She rattled off the household rules she promised to enforce: no drugs or alcohol, Natalie had to keep her room clean, wash Judy's clothes, feed and bathe her, et cetera. When Children's Aid objected, Victoria said, "When you pay my rent, my utilities, my phone, or any other bills I have, then you can come in and tell me who can come into my home and who not." The judge, Victoria said, snickered and ruled: "Permission granted for you to take your granddaughter home!"

Before a month was up, though, the police and Children's Aid had to remove Natalie from the house. Sometimes, she would fall asleep in a bathtub full of water with Judy in her arms, and Victoria would have to take the child away from her. One evening, Victoria went out for a few hours and left her husband at home with Natalie and Judy. "The baby started crying. Natalie shook that child so hard my husband thought the child's eyeballs were going to fall out! So I reported it to Children's Aid. I told them, 'She is not to be trusted with her.'"

When Natalie came around again a few months later, Victoria warned her not to say anything to Children's Aid.

Victoria said, "You get into a fight with them, you're going to lose everything." Victoria hardly paused for breath before she told me, "When Children's Aid came, boy she was ready for them, I'm telling you! She blasted them. The two of them got into it in the middle of my kitchen. Natalie had Judy in her arms. She walked back and forth two or three times. She almost hit Judy's head against the wall! The worker said to her, 'Give me that child.' Natalie said, 'Yeah, I'll give you a slap in the mouth!' " Victoria watched them go at it for about twenty minutes, then stood up and said, "Natalie, give me the baby, because if you hurt that baby, I'm telling you in the presence of the worker here, I'll be hurting you. That child is in my care, not yours."

Then Natalie got on the computer to email her mother—Victoria's daughter—and she stayed on it, which tied up the telephone line. The worker wanted to call her supervisor but couldn't because she had to use that phone. So Victoria unplugged the computer, the worker made the call, and in ten minutes two police officers came. Victoria phoned Natalie's mother, Bridget, and said they'd be dropping Natalie off at a gas station for Bridget to pick up. Then Victoria handed the phone to the police officer. She said, "After that, Bridget was giving me hell. She thought she was talking to me on the phone. She was talking to the cop! He was hearing the threats and everything else she was throwing at me. Finally, he says to her, 'You are not talking to your mother, you know; you are talking to constable so and so.'" They took Natalie away in handcuffs.

"From that day on," Victoria said, "I haven't even spoken to her. She won't have anything to do with me."

Natalie's problems, she said, began in childhood. Bridget was addicted to drugs and alcohol, and when they were teenagers, Natalie and her sister, on their own initiative, asked the court to make them wards of the Crown. Since then, the two of them were in and out of foster and group homes.

I asked Victoria if she's ever felt guilt or shame about how she raised Bridget, or that she has three generations of troubled children in her family. "I asked myself more than once about that," she replied. "Where did I go wrong? But she was the only one out of ten! All the others: beautiful homes, beautiful jobs. They were all treated the same way!"

When Judy was born, Victoria said, "Bridget's the one who came crying to me, 'Mom, don't let Children's Aid go in and take the baby!' She said it'd break her heart to let them take the child. So I went straight to the hospital. I asked Natalie what did she want me to do. She started to cry, 'Don't let 'em take my baby....If I have to, I'll sign her over to you till I'm eighteen'—which was only two months away." Victoria told me, "I was very angry. To be honest, I was angry that her mother—my daughter—wasn't even allowed to go into the hospital to visit them, because Children's Aid wouldn't allow her there." Children's Aid seemed to have Bridget on a blacklist. Victoria wasn't sure why, but she suspected it was a lot more than Bridget's being "a damn poor housekeeper....I always said I wouldn't put my cat in there, the place was so filthy."

Bridget fought Victoria repeatedly in court. She claimed Victoria was an unfit caregiver. "I have a box more than a foot high of papers for being hauled to court," Victoria said. "She had a friend of hers do up papers to send to me, and everything they put in them was lies."

Once, she said, the police came to her door with a warrant to search her house. "You don't need a warrant to search my house, buddy," Victoria told the officer. "He looked at me and said, 'I knew you'd say that.' But he said they reported me as having drugs. The cops came in, took the cushions off my chesterfield, took the covers off the cushions....They wanted to look under the beds. I said, 'Go ahead, but you make sure you put everything back as you found it.'" They found nothing. After the baby came, she didn't allow anyone even to smoke tobacco in the house, not even her husband.

While raising Natalie, Victoria also cared for her husband after he was diagnosed with Alzheimer's. Three years before I met her, they sold their summer cottage and moved to a larger centre where they could get psychiatric help, anger management, and special schooling for Judy that they couldn't get before.

Judy's anger, Victoria told me, is FASD-related. "When she was born, she used to do an awful lot of screaming and crying. Being an old-fashioned mother, I thought she was colicky. Her mother was breastfeeding her. So I was trying to get her mother to give up drinking Pepsi, because

Pepsi is really gassy. Nope, she says. She wasn't changing her life for nobody."

After Natalie went away, when Judy was just a baby, Victoria said she'd often be driving Judy somewhere, and Judy would scream, flail her arms around in a frenzy, and pick off chunks of her own skin. Victoria would pull off and walk along the side of the road for hours with her to settle her down. "One day," Victoria said, "I hauled into the Canadian Tire parking lot and she was screaming her head off. This fella came along with his wife, and he said, 'If I had her, I'd give her a good ass-slapping!' I said, 'Yeah? You wait until you find out what's the matter with the child before you talk like that. There's something seriously wrong with this child, and it's because the mother was into drugs and alcohol before she was born!'"

When Judy was 3 months old, Victoria finally found a pediatrician who knew FASD. "He says to me, 'Has this child been diagnosed with anything?' I said, 'No. That's why I'm here.' He says, 'Were drugs and alcohol involved before this child's birth?' I said, 'Yes. Lots of it.' He said, 'I thought so. I'm going to send her to a real specialist to find out, but I'm almost certain this child has FASD.' I said, 'What's FASD?' I hadn't a clue. He said, 'Fetal alcohol and drug syndrome.' I said, I thought she was colicky and was giving her sugar water to calm her down. He said, 'Omigod, mum! Don't do that anymore! Do you not realize an alcoholic needs sugar?' " Though Judy had been born an alcoholic, it would take three more years to get the official FASD diagnosis.

In a court appearance after Victoria found out about FASD, the judge confronted Natalie. Natalie said, "I never did drugs. I never did alcohol." "The judge," Victoria explained, "looked at her and said, 'Sit down, young lady. Don't you stand up here and lie to me. If that child did not get it from you, I'm damn well sure she didn't get it from great-grandma, cause she didn't carry her! You did!'" After the diagnosis, Victoria got $420 a month from ODS,[2] but before her husband retired, it was less than a hundred. They also got a child tax credit of $69.76 a month, but no other government support—no drug coverage, and nothing to help pay for gatherings like the CANGRANDS camp.

Victoria said she tried three Ritalin-related drugs on Judy, but all of them "set her crazy." When Judy was three, Victoria had her placed in daycare but she soon had to be moved to a private facility with one-on-one supervision. "She would bite pieces of flesh to bring blood, not only out of herself but out of the other kids. She would pull the hair off their heads, big fistfuls of it. She could be walking along, one of them could be sitting down and had something she wanted. She wouldn't ask for it, she'd just slap them across the face. They'd drop it and she'd pick it up." Victoria shudders at the memory. "Oh! It was beyond control!"

She went to another pediatrician and tried another drug. The doctor said it worked wonders for other kids.

---

2   Ontario Disability Support.

But it wasn't covered by any drug plan, and it was expensive. "If you think it will help that child," Victoria told him, "you let me worry about the cost." Even now, with the medication, "she can sit down and pull chunks out of her face, pull chunks out of her arm until the blood runs through. Her legs, she'll sit down and pick the flesh right off!" Victoria sighed and said, "But it was worse before."

Then she told me about their 14-year-old dog. "She loved that dog, but she was cruel." Once, Judy had the dog under the kitchen table and kept stabbing it with a fork. Another time, she picked the dog up and threw it against the wall. It got so bad that Victoria phoned the crisis centre for help. Then the dog started having epileptic fits and had to be euthanized.

After they got Judy to a psychiatrist and increased her medication, Judy said she wanted a kitten. "We said no, you're not getting any kitten! Not until you show us you can take care of it and be gentle to it." But Judy nagged them for a kitten. Then, for two months she stopped nagging. Victoria decided to make an agreement with her: Judy would clean the litter box, feed the kitten, give her water, and do everything to look after her. Judy got the kitten for her ninth birthday, Victoria said, and, "Boy, just like that, she was up at six in the morning, had that cat ready and got herself ready for school....It was the greatest therapy we ever gave her." Before the kitten, Judy couldn't read her own name; two months later, "she could take down any kind of book, and sit down and read it." So the school took her out of the special class she was in and put her in the regular grade 3 class. "She got top marks!" Victoria said. "You should see her report card!" She always has a book in her hands, and she's always "reading, reading, reading."

At this point in our conversation, a grandparent—a retired school principal—stood near the cafeteria door and swung a handbell back and forth to ring us all in for supper. Just like the nuns used to do after recess at Queen of the Holy Rosary School when I was in elementary school over fifty years ago: a shiny, flared brass bell with a dark brown wooden spindle for a handle. I knew we had a few minutes before the kids stopped bouncing the basketball, operating backhoes in the sandbox, and swimming in the pool, so I asked Victoria if she had just one wish for herself and all the grandparents in Canada who raise grandchildren.

"I wish the government would smarten up," she said, with the same icy voice and clenched jaw she used to talk about the social workers and lawyers she fought in court. "And help seniors who are looking after those kids and give them some real support instead of us having to fight for everything. And recognize what we're doing!"

I added, "And how much we're saving society." She nodded and said, "If they'd only stop and realize that. 'Oh well, your responsibility—not ours.' I've had that said to me so often! They used to make me angry, and I'd just stand up and tell them off and walk out."

She shuddered and shook her head as if to rid herself of an infestation of head lice masquerading as civil servants, politicians, and better-than-thou passersby. "I've often told them, 'I hope to God you're never in the same position.' I told them many times, 'Where's the money coming from to keep you in a job?' It's people like us. It's our tax dollars. If there weren't people like us to go to them with things, what would they want a job for? If you were a social worker, and nobody needed social assistance or help, why would you have a job? And we're getting half the health care! The things you really want, you can't get coverage for."

I couldn't find an estimate of how much Kinship Care parents—most of them grandparents—save Canadian government agencies by keeping children out of foster care and prisons and off the streets, but a US source estimates that our American counterparts save the taxpayer $6.5 billion each year.[3] Child welfare departments are the mechanism communities set up to backstop families that can't care for their own, but in jurisdictions of 4 million (Alberta), 13 million (Ontario), or even 148,000 (Prince Edward Island), the economies of scale overwhelm the economies of personhood. Governments fund child welfare not because they want to help children, and certainly not because they love them, but primarily to avoid bad publicity when, for example, a child in care dies, and they want to do it as cheaply and as impersonally as possible.

Many grandparents simply avoid social workers and the entire child welfare system. Some say, "This is my grandson,

---

3   Brandon Gaille, "23 Statistics on Grandparents Raising Grandchildren," https://brandongaille.com/21-statistics-on-grandparents-raising-grandchildren/.

and I can take care of him myself! He's family!" Others feel they've failed as parents and withdraw from society. Still others are afraid child welfare will take the kids away and they'll never see them again. Grandparents like these are invisible. They aren't included in statistics, and they're almost impossible to contact. I was lucky to discover Trina. She lives a few blocks away from me. I'd worked with her in a couple of community organizations, but I didn't know she was raising her granddaughter until I volunteered to be a cashier for our community league's biennial casino.

TWO

Child Welfare: Keep Out!

The nine scariest words in the English language:
I'm from the government and I'm here to help.
                                        —*Ronald Reagan*

I wouldn't wish dealing with the Children's
Services department on my worst enemy.
                                        —*Trina*

I sat behind the cashier's counter at the Yellowhead Casino and looked through bulletproof glass at flashing blue, yellow, and red lights. Row after row of slot machines, with a person sitting in front of about every tenth one. Things were dead slow on the 11:00 a.m. to 7:00 p.m. shift. In the cashier's room, the continuous whiz-bang, ding-ding-ding of the slots was as muffled and distant as the pinball machines I remember from the 1960s.

Back then, I'd insert a nickel and thwack a shiny steel ball out of a chute and watch it light up 50, 100, 500 point bonuses as it hit spring-loaded obstacles and rang bell after bell, lights flashing as gravity pulled it down to the exit hole next to me. I'd push a flipper button to shoot it up again and rack up more points. I'd watch my fifth steel ball roll out of play and wait for my score to tally up. One game out of maybe twenty, I'd win a free game. But the people here in the Yellowhead Casino kept dropping cash in the slot, hoping for a handful of loonies or the big jackpot, even though the odds were stacked against them.

The electronic door lock buzzed, and Trina bounded in, laughing and smiling as if she'd just won a million dollars. I looked behind me and said hi. Trina said her daughter would be volunteering about 3:00 p.m. "This is the first time I've gotten her out to do much of anything!" She assumed everyone in the room knew why this was a big deal. I didn't. Not until a week later, when she joined me at Tony's Pizza for lunch. We sat at a table in the back corner, away from the TVs that streamed hockey and soccer game reruns, away from the constant lunch-hour chatter and traffic. Trina was jovial, laughing and smiling as she said hello and sat down.

"When the first grandchild was born," she said, "my daughter Marlene was living in one of the boys and girls housing programs. The day she gave birth she was evicted from the program! She was 16. They had rules and regulations that had to be followed. I didn't have a part in that program because she'd been apprehended, and that was the path child welfare chose for her." Marlene is now 28 and on permanent disability because of the damage drug addiction did to her. Trina has raised Marlene's first child, Leeanne, for the first twelve years of her life. Leeanne was the first of four babies Marlene couldn't raise.

At the age of 14, Marlene was raped. Trina pressed charges, and the rapist went to prison for a few years. But Trina and her family got a life sentence. It was as if he'd murdered Marlene and given Trina somebody else in her place. After the rape, Marlene acted out so badly that Trina called child welfare for help. She was desperate. She knew child welfare had access to treatment programs she didn't. "That's not what they did," she said. Trina gritted her teeth and clenched her fists on the tabletop. "They came in and apprehended her!" For two years, Trina said, she got the odd, brief phone call from Marlene, but child welfare didn't tell her what decisions they made or anything that was happening with Marlene. Trina discovered later that for those two years, Marlene believed Trina had called child welfare to take her away, that Trina had abandoned her.

"Leeanne was born on June 25, and on June 26 Marlene was evicted," Trina told me. Her voice dropped lower and her words came more slowly, but her eyes flashed sparks from a fire deep inside. "She was in hospital and had absolutely no place to go! What kind of program evicts a kid who's sixteen and leaves her standing on the street corner with a brand new baby?" Trina said she had no choice but to take Marlene and baby Leeanne home.

When Leeanne was 6 or 7 months old, Trina said, "Marlene asked if I would watch Leeanne so she could go for coffee with some friends." Trina picked up her glass of water, sipped, and forced a chuckle. "The next phone call I got was the next morning at 2:00 a.m. from the Royal Alexandra Hospital. She'd been brought in with a drug overdose, and they were releasing her. Three, four months after that, she walked out the door." Not quite 17, Marlene was profoundly addicted.

Trina applied for legal custody of Leeanne, but child welfare blocked her, and she had to get a court order before they would give her any information they had about Marlene. When they did, it was a file two inches thick. Child welfare applied to be an intervener in the case, but Trina told the judge, "With all due respect, Your Honour, if the department had done their job in the first place, I wouldn't be standing here today! I don't want any part of the department in this order!"

Trina won that battle. She was free to raise Leeanne on her own, without government interference. That was in 2004, when the Alberta government rewrote legislation related to children in care, creating the new kinship program. It was also the year Marlene gave birth to twins.

Marlene was in and out of a safe house that year, trying to stay clean. When she gave birth, the hospital notified child welfare because Marlene was so young and obviously addicted. Trina worked with child welfare because that was the only way to get help for Marlene. Trina took Marlene and the babies home with her until she could figure out what to do. On November 11, just a week after giving birth, Marlene walked away, totally overwhelmed by the twins.

"On December 2, child welfare finally called the house and wanted to know how things were going," Trina said. "I said things are going fine. I'm going to court tomorrow to get a guardianship order." With their mother gone, nobody had legal authority to make decisions for the babies, and Trina wasn't about to give them over to child welfare. She laughed as she told this part of the story; she's a positive person and apparently decided long ago that, at this point in her life, laughter is healthier than tears. Or maybe she simply ran out of tears.

Trina decided she couldn't raise 3-year-old Leeanne and the twins, but she was never going to give the twins up completely, so she looked for someone to adopt them. She insisted that it was not a *decision* to have an open, private adoption: "It was a *demand!*" She said people have to have roots, especially children as damaged as these grandchildren of hers.

Even though she had a full-time job and a part-time job too, Trina worked with child welfare to find an adoptive family. Child welfare gave her help with daycare, but that, too, was a battle. "They wanted me to haul a set of twins to daycare every day in the dead of winter," Trina said. "I told them to bite me! They could pay for somebody to come into my house!" When child welfare finally relented, the babysitter was not allowed to look after Leeanne. So Trina took her to daycare on her way to work. She also fought with child welfare to pay for diapers and milk for the twins, which cost nearly a thousand dollars a month. "Never mind the clothes, the basinets, the laundry, keeping the heat up because there's these teeny, tiny babies, and car seats, blah, blah, blah! *And, it's the dead of winter!*"

This arrangement continued for six months: seven days a week, 5:00 a.m. to midnight, Trina working two jobs, three kids under three. It wore me out just to imagine it. When did she sleep?

Trina ran into more problems with child welfare on the adoption. A social worker trying to "help," Trina said, "phoned me at work one day and said, 'Call your babysitter; we're coming to pick up the twins. I found a foster-to-adopt home.' Right in the middle of the day at work! I said, 'No! I would advise you not to go onto my property.'"

Eventually, Trina found a helpful adoption worker and a family who already had one adopted child. Trina was happy about that, and she's had a long and close relationship with the family since then. But when she realized child welfare was paying the adopting family's expenses, she was furious. "Here's the birth family willing to do whatever we need to do for the children," she told me, "and we're not offered a penny of help. So you put the children up for adoption and you find out that this family is given a cheque for over $3,000 a month for the three kids, and everything is paid for—medication, glasses, respite care, extracurricular activities. Not a single penny comes out of their pocket to support those children!"

Trina struggled to control the pitch and volume of her voice. I imagined us in a soundproof room and her yelling so loudly that my eyebrows tickled and I had to turn off my hearing aids. That's how much anger she carried. She held a forkful of penne dripping with Bolognese sauce about two inches above her plate and looked down at it, as if the world it lived in was out of her reach. The cadence of her speech ratcheted up and up as she spoke. "I think of all the bingos I had to work for Leeanne's dancing, all the body suits and tap shoes and jazz shoes and hip-hop shoes and everything I've taken out of my pocket. The adoptive mother gets reimbursed!"

When she remembered the good times, her voice was melodious and fluid, like the opening of Beethoven's *Pastoral* Symphony. She described "watching those babies grow and do things. When I was home I put them down on a blanket on the floor. I'd give them exercises to strengthen their legs. They were adorable." She scowled again and added, "But that's a hard job." Her voice now sounded more like the ominous Pum-Pum-Pum *PUMMM* at the start of Beethoven's 5th.

"But what about that fourth child?" I ask. "You just said you gave three up for adoption, but you kept Leeanne." She told me that Marlene's addiction got even worse after she left the twins behind. She took stronger and stronger drugs to dull the guilt of abandoning three children and to bury the shame of addiction itself. When Marlene met the father of her fourth baby, she was living on the street. "The little boy was born, I think it was a Friday night," Trina said. "They discharged her on Saturday." The baby was tiny, clearly addicted, and spent a lot of time in the neonatal unit. Child welfare apprehended him immediately.

The people who adopted the twins adopted him too. They phoned child welfare and didn't have to go through the courts. Trina said she never had custody of him, but "I was at the hospital every single night until they discharged him to the adoptive parents."

Two weeks after giving birth, while the baby was still in the Royal Alexandra Hospital, Marlene had a brain aneurism. Trina went back and forth every day for several months between the Royal Alexandra Hospital, where the baby was, and the brain trauma unit of the University of Alberta Hospital, to visit her daughter. "He was sick and the adoptive mother needed me. The idea wasn't to find somebody to adopt him and then disappear. And I had to see my child! Brain aneurisms are dangerous and leave a lot of cognitive issues behind," she said. "The aneurism was life-threatening, but it put her on the path to rehab and stable housing."

That fourth baby, though, has long-term issues, Trina said. He's spent time in the intensive care unit at the Stollery Children's Hospital. He had trouble swallowing, and even now, everything he eats has to be thickened. "He can't enjoy watermelon unless it's all squished up and you put thickener in it," she says. "He's six or seven now."

Because these were open adoptions, Trina could maintain relationships with all three children, but as a grandmother, not a parent. They've had frequent visits and shared photographs. She even got a video-recorded birthday message where the kids all sang "Happy Birthday, Gramma!"

Trina has kept closely connected with Marlene through everything, even when the relationship was one-sided and she got nothing back. She noted that people on disability pensions hardly get enough for necessities, "So I always made sure that if they ran out of food, I would help them pick up a few things." She's often given Marlene "pop bottles and cans and juice jugs and stuff" she can take to the bottle depot for cigarette money and other things.

Marlene and the father of the youngest child have lived together for nine years and have been on methadone for six, Trina said, but both are so damaged they can't work even part-time. She's tried to introduce them to new things, like volunteering at the casino. Their tendency has been to withdraw, because they know that when they get triggered, the next relapse is only a breath away. And for them, triggers are everywhere. Trina said Marlene soon turns 30, but emotionally she's only half that age. And it all started with that rape and child welfare's interference.

Leeanne, who was 12 when Trina and I talked, visited Marlene almost every day after school. But Trina told me that, whenever Leeanne spent much time there, she'd come home and say, "I'm really glad I have you. I'm really glad you kept me, Grandma."

At this point in our conversation, I marveled at Trina's resilience. I remembered the self-care analogy they use in caregiver groups. It references the routine speech given prior to every passenger aircraft takeoff, the speech almost nobody listens to anymore. It tells people traveling with children that, when the oxygen masks pop out, "Put your own on first!" If caregivers don't take care of themselves, they are no use to anybody. I wondered: where is Trina's oxygen mask? And so I asked her, "What do you do to take care of yourself?"

She told me she's often wished for a grandparents support group in Edmonton where she could talk openly about her life with people who've been there. She told me of the network of friends she has, people she has worked with, her other daughters and relatives, how they've all pitched in to help her. She told me she used to work for the Centre to End All Sexual Exploitation, and that every January she organizes a dinner for former prostitutes who struggle to feed themselves and their families. She said that gives her energy, even though it's a lot of work. She also loves to do volunteer work to make the community better. Along the way, she networks with people like me, and often gets free tickets to things she can't afford. At the casino that we worked together, a friend of hers came to give her six show tickets for the following Friday and six more for the Friday after. That's Trina's formula for self-care on a tight budget.

When Leeanne was little, though, self-care was a luxury Trina couldn't afford. She rarely went out. After a while, Trina got Leeanne's aunts to babysit now and then. Once Marlene was doing better, she could come over sometimes to help. But now that Leeanne's older, Trina laughed, "It's all about me. I've given everything I've got to everybody else, and if I'm going to croak, I'm not going to croak sitting on the couch whining and crying. I'm going to be out having fun!" Along the way, she got plenty back from Leeanne herself. "Leeanne keeps me alive," Trina said. "She keeps me young. She gives me something to look forward to every single day." They have a good relationship, but with Leeanne on the cusp of being a teenager, Trina flinched at the prospect of puberty, hormones, boys hanging around. "That could change quickly!"

Leeanne and Trina have both found comfort in two dogs they've had part-time. The dogs belong to Trina's daughter Ashleigh, who lives in Trina's basement and is happy to share. The 8-year-old dog doesn't like children, except for Leeanne. He's "a nipper," and he's bitten everybody but Leeanne. Trina said the other one is a burrowing dog, little taller than a Shih Tzu. "If I'm not out of bed in the morning, he comes upstairs and crawls under the blankets. Just digs in there. Keeps the bed warm!" She laughed. "Unconditional love," she called it.

At this point in the conversation, I realized: Trina talked about her social life, her daughters, her grandkids; I've seen her out in the community, but I haven't seen or heard anything about her husband. She said she's 57 years old. Retirement couldn't be far away, I assumed, so I asked what plans she and her husband had. "I'm working on my Freedom 85 plan," she laughed. "In my retirement I'm going to live in the same abject poverty I've lived in all my life." Peter, she said, left three years ago—eleven years after the rape, when Leeanne was 9 and the other three children were long gone. Their relationship was 32 years old when it died.

When they bought their small, two-story duplex infill home in inner-city Edmonton, it was going to be just the two of them. They dreamt of retiring there. But Peter had had enough. Maybe he felt that to care for himself he had to get away. When he left, Trina had heart problems so severe she thought she was dying. The doctors showed her an image of her heart. She said pieces of it were simply missing. Volunteer work, she said, "fills up the empty holes." She fills them with laughter too. She laughed long and hard in Tony's Pizza as she recalled the time just after Peter left. She told me she ripped all the sheets off their bed and threw them in the garbage. For weeks, every night she curled up in a blanket, on the bare mattress, and cried herself to sleep. Then she got rid of all her furniture and replaced it with things that didn't remind her of Peter, their previous life, their hopes for retirement.

Trina tried one therapist after another until she found one who did body therapy, which focused on the connection between grief and physical health. The therapist said a key step in the process is to name the pain. At the time, Trina had hemorrhoids so painful that for three months she couldn't even sit up straight; she had a desk job and had to sit on one cheek at a time to type. She said it was "the worst case of hemorrhoids I ever had." She decided to name the hemorrhoids Peter, "because he was the biggest pain in the ass!" She roared with laughter as she said this, and I laughed loud and hard too. I'm sure everyone in Tony's turned their heads around to look at us.

Okay. She named the pain. But the hemorrhoids still hurt like hell. To take her mind off them, she and a friend went out for an evening of bar wrestling. "We got these appetizers," she said. "Little steak bits wrapped in bacon." She closed her eyes and smiled as her tongue remembered the taste. Greasy, salty smoked bacon. Juicy, grilled beef. Yumm! "Red meat," she said. "Not supposed to eat that when you have hemorrhoids!" She laughed again. "You're not supposed to have bacon either! But I ate 'em anyway, they were so-o-o-o good!" So she ordered seconds and ate some more. "I was sure I was gonna die, and it was gonna be horrible," but she was happy to pay the price to escape the pain for just one night. But she didn't die. Those things should have worsened her condition, but they didn't. Instead, the hemorrhoids went away. And Trina claimed it was all because she named them Peter.

But the bigger pain never goes away. The hole in Trina's heart. The daughter whose life the rapist shattered, the one Marlene can never be again after so many years living on the street, doing drugs. "It rips you in half!" Trina said, her voice as near to breaking as I've ever heard it. "*You can't breathe*," she whispered.

In 2005, when Marlene was most active working the streets, Trina worked for the Prostitution Action and Awareness Foundation of Edmonton (PAAFE).[1] That year four prostitutes were murdered in Edmonton. A young woman's body was found on a nearby golf course. The

---

1 PAAFE has since then been renamed the Centre to End All Sexual Exploitation (CEASE).

brutal murder was the lead story in newspapers and on radio and television for several days before the police could confirm it was Nina Courtepatte. It could have been any young woman. When the body was still unidentified, two police officers came to the PAAFE office with pictures of the body to see if anyone could identify the victim. Trina recalled that day vividly. One officer showed pictures to others in the office, and "the other officer was with me on the couch, with his phone on speed dial to 9-1-1 because I was hyperventilating so badly. He was convinced I was going to have a heart attack. I thought it was my kid!"

As she told the story ten years later, she groaned from deep in her gut, but still she held back the tears. "You don't hear from them! *You don't know where they are!*" When Trina and I spoke in Tony's Pizza, Marlene had been in a stable relationship for years and had been drug-free for a long time. "But," Trina said, "if the phone rings after nine o'clock, my heart stops. Still does." She added, "Lots of nights I go to bed crying. But what can you do to make it different?"

I picked up the bill, and we walked toward the door. "This isn't the plan I had for my life," she chuckled. "Raising children at age fifty-seven?" But she's been doing it on her own and at her own expense, without child welfare's support or interference. As our conversation ended, she was glad that she'd shared her story with a kindred spirit. She said, "I always thought there should be a place for grandparents, a little coffee group or something where we could just have a safe place to complain." I thought so too. The only one I found in Edmonton met once a month, on a Tuesday night. I couldn't go because we'd have to find a babysitter, and the budget was tight. Then I stumbled across a group in rural Alberta, and I wondered, "Why aren't there more of these in the big cities?" I knew I was too busy and worn down to organize one, and I was sure most skipped-generation grandparents felt the same way. So I mustered enough energy to take several trips to the country and see how a grandparent support group works.

THREE

The Pride of Grandparents: A Support Group Meets

Other people have no concept of what we're going
through. This group helped us pull through a lot
of bad times. It's given us an outlet where we can
talk and be ourselves, and people understand.

—*A grandmother*

Except for the plywood wheelchair ramp, this brown brick building in rural Alberta could be Queen of the Holy Rosary School in Overland Park, Kansas, where I graduated from grade 8 in 1962. It's about the same age I am: 67. It's slated for demolition. The grandparenting group meets here every Friday morning from September to June. Today, the four couples and eight women present are themselves in various stages of demolition. Some of this is aging, but most of it is the emotional, physical, and financial stress of raising a second generation of children. All are here to renovate themselves enough to survive the next week. For one of the women, this is her first meeting.

The furniture is old too. A pair of low-slung, glossy, greyish-brown vinyl chesterfields have gaudy bright yellow, blue, and green throw pillows placed on them at regular intervals. With a dozen grey vinyl chairs, they form a large, flat-sided circle in the centre of what had once been a classroom for fifty students.

Inside are pale beige walls, brown Formica-top tables, worn-through grey linoleum, faded blue jeans, ragged sweaters, scuffed-up winter boots, white hair, bald heads, double chins. Outside the west-facing windows, low-lying black clouds drift above crusts of dirty, end-of-winter snow. A four-by-twelve-foot sheet of newsprint is taped to the south wall, where a blackboard used to be. It says "ABORIGINAL DAY 2013" in large, stenciled black letters across the centre; the rest is a mosaic of children's blue, green, red, yellow, orange, purple, and black handprints pointing in all directions.

This group started eight years ago. Two social workers organize it and keep it going. They spread refreshments out on one of the tables every week. Grandparents with preschool-aged children can leave them from 9:30 to noon, for free, at the daycare down the hall. For that reason, meetings usually end at noon. At 9:30, most grandparents are in their seats. Some nestle steaming cups of coffee or tea in their hands. Some balance plates of fresh strawberries, grapes, brownies, or cheese and crackers on their knees.

The normal routine when there's a first-timer is to go around once so everyone can summarize their family history. Then the group does two more rounds. The first is a check-in: everyone takes five minutes or so to talk about what's happened in their lives since the last meeting. A social worker–facilitator then asks each one if he or she wants feedback. At the end of the check-in, we go around the circle again, and the floor is open for feedback and discussion.

In order to create a more cohesive narrative of a sample meeting, and to keep each family's experiences together, I've collapsed the first two rounds into one. For this meeting, everybody agrees I can record their words, as long as I change names to protect the children's privacy. My phone, with the voice recorder turned on, becomes our talking stick.

Julie, the facilitator, asks who'd like to start.

Mary immediately reaches for the phone. "My husband and I got our four grandsons two and a half years ago," she says. "I called the child abuse hotline. The dad was removed from the home. My daughter, who'd just found out she was pregnant with number four, was left in the house with three boys aged 3, 2, and 3 months. The fourth was born two and a half months premature. It got to be too much for her. She surrendered them to Children's Services. She said to me, 'Can you keep them for the weekend?' " Several people chuckle: they, too, took their grandkids in "for the weekend."

"They've been here ever since," Mary continues. "But we're lucky, because we have full funding through

Children's Services. We're a Kinship Care home, but we're in the process of adopting. We live in a little thousand-square-foot house. Our house is full and busy and noisy—" She pauses, crosses her legs, and forces a smile. "For the most part, they're good boys, but they all suffer from the same things. I don't know if their mom was drinking when she had them. I don't know if they were fed properly. Mick, the oldest, I think was responsible for the two littler ones for a long time. Mom would say, 'Get up. Turn on a movie. Get whatever you want to eat out of the cupboard.' The second oldest one, trying to get him off TV when they first came was almost like getting him off heroin. It was terrible. Terrible! He'd have meltdowns and cry when you didn't turn on the TV.

"My husband doesn't come to this group very often," Mary adds, "because he has his own business now. He's my second husband. Never had children of his own. He thinks this is wonderful! He gets to play with little kids! 'Cause he's really just a big kid." She laughs. "But I tell him constantly, 'No, you can't do that! Because they're impressionable at that age. You need to set boundaries now, because if you don't, they won't get the concept when they're ten.'"

She says, "I had five children. They're all adults now. This is déjà vu!" She laughs. "But I'm lucky. One of my sons and his wife live close by. They help a lot. I haven't seen my daughter, their mom, for over a year—" She takes a quick breath. Her chest heaves. She shakes her head to settle her nerves. "Mick said to me this morning, 'Pretty soon I'm gonna call you mom.'

"I thought you were gonna call me 'gramma' forever," she says. "But I guess we'll let them call us whatever they want."

Mary says she's had a good week. Nick, her oldest, has five stitches in his eyebrow, and now the girls in grade 1 and 2 feel sorry for him. His school had International Night, she says, and the teachers, classmates—everybody—gave him lots of attention.

"Oh! I totally forgot!" she says. "I should call the health unit to get the stitches out." She pauses for a second to reconsider. "But maybe I'll just do it myself." She notes that the indoor soccer season is over, and that she won't have to drive kids to games and practice four times a week. Yay! At least until spring soccer. She says her family started a new practice in the home, "an attitude of gratitude, so when we get up in the morning, we think of something good that's happening rather than complaining about what we don't have." Julie asks her if she'd like feedback. "I don't need it," Mary says, "unless you have something."

Mary passes the "talking stick" to Vicky and Greg. Vicki starts: "Eight years now we've had Nancy and Tom. Nancy is my son's daughter. They have the same mom. They were in foster care since Nancy was two months old. Tom is seven years older than her. Their mom, my son also—" Vicky pauses. She inhales slowly, looks at the floor. "Alcohol. Nancy was born with crack cocaine in her system. No sign of damage right now. They're both doing very well. Tom's always done well in school, basketball, sports, all kinds of things. He's seventeen now. I hope he's making all the right choices like he always has. And ten-year-old Nancy's just fun. She's been dancing, doing all kinds of crafts, voice, piano, soccer, friends. She loves her friends. But we always think: what's around the corner?

"For quite a while, we didn't see the parents," she says. "My son lives in Edmonton now. Neither of them wants the kids back. Their mom has gone through rehab and is into a new relationship and had another girl. She had a boy while the kids were in care, and he went straight to foster care. The kids don't ask about the parents. If they're there, it's good. If they call, it's good. They don't voice very much about that, but I'm sure it's on their minds." She offers the "stick" to Greg and asks, "Anything else?"

Greg takes it and says, "This is our second marriage. We got to the point almost where we were going to retire, and God kind of laughed at us." He smiles. Everybody laughs. "In the first part of our relationship, we helped a long time with one of my grandchildren and Vicky's, out on the farm. That made it easy for us to jump into this when these kids came our way."

He turns toward Vicky and grimaces. "We face a little calamity coming up on the weekend." Tom, their 17-year-old, is going to an overnight party with his basketball team, and they pray everything is going to be okay. Vicky says Tom's girlfriend is only a "friend" now. She's relieved about that. Somebody across the circle says, "There'll be another one!" Vicky laughs. "Yeah. Waiting in line." Greg chuckles, "Hopefully the next one won't be sucking on his neck!" Everybody laughs.

Vicky wonders if Greg will be as eager to give permission for Nancy to go to an overnight party at age seventeen as he was for Tom. Vicky says she went into Nancy's room the other day and found "every bit of clothing out of the closet, on the floor—cleaning up!" And Nancy said, "It's going to be spring and summer soon; I'm gonna get rid of some of this old stuff." Before Julie can ask, Vicky laughs and says, "If there's any feedback, fine."

She passes the phone to April. Her husband, Luke, sits to her left, wearing a sweat-soaked, broad-brimmed Australian outback-style leather hat he never takes off. "We're raising our seven-year-old grandson, Eric. We've had him since he was seven months old," April says. "He was living with his mother and our son. They were both into abuse of alcohol, drugs, what have you. She said she didn't drink during pregnancy, but we know of at least two times she did. A neighbour reported them, and Eric was picked up by child welfare." April and Luke got a call in the middle of the night telling them to come to downtown Edmonton to pick him up.

"Like most of us here," April says, "we hoped the parents could be parents someday, but that has never happened." Her voice breaks. She reaches for Luke's hand and squeezes. "Now we've lost our son!" She moans and takes a deep breath. "Just before Eric's second birthday, he committed suicide. A year later—" April's breathing morphs into a staccato of whimpers. She clenches her eyes shut. "Eric's mom was killed in a car accident." Someone picks up a box of tissues from the other side of the room and rushes it over to her.

April pulls out a tissue and daubs both eyes. "We have private guardianship," she says. "It's permanent. Nobody to go back to." I feel my own heart stuttering. April's grief catches in my throat and tears well up in my eyes. I look around. All the smiles have disappeared.

"It's been very hard," April says, "for Eric and us. We've had aides help him, preschool and kindergarten." She takes another deep breath, daubs more tears, and says, "He's come a long way. He's doing pretty good now. He's in grade 2. The supports have made a big difference in all our lives." Her chest heaves. Luke puts his arm around her. Several people wipe tears on their sleeves. Everyone looks at the floor. The room is silent as a tomb.

When April's breathing is under control again, she says her week was full of doctors' appointments. She was on a machine to monitor her blood pressure for twenty-four hours. Yesterday morning, while getting Eric ready for school, the phone rang. It was a neighbour with a medical emergency. So April called an ambulance, and after it came and took the neighbour away, she drove his two kids to school. After school, April and Luke had those kids again, and this morning they took three kids to school. The neighbour was still in the hospital. She called some friends to help. She's had the kids twenty-four hours but thinks she has somebody to take them for the weekend so she can have a break.

"They're basically good kids," she says, "but it's difficult to keep them under control. It isn't good for Eric, either," she complains. "These kids never do anything on their own! I tell them, 'Can you get washed up?' and they say, 'Can you help me?' " She tells them, "No. I'll put water in here for you, and you wash up." She wonders how she can brush every tooth, make breakfast, prepare lunches, and all the rest. "But it's just gonna have to work," she says.

April pauses, and Julie asks, "Is there anything else?" April says, "*Isn't that enough?*" Everybody laughs. Cindy asks, "How's *that* affecting your blood pressure?" A few people chuckle.

Luke, who hasn't said anything all day, mumbles in his deep, Johnny Cash–like, crushed-gravel-backroad-sounding voice: "I phoned the hospital. Doesn't sound too good."

Julie asks if they want feedback. Luke growls, "No," and passes the "stick" to Colleen.

Colleen says she's the single grandmother of John and has no family support nearby. "John's father is my son," she says. "His mother has never been a mother to him. From day one, they lived in my home. Social services showed up at our door two weeks ago when I was here, at the meeting. They threatened to take John if I didn't move out with him." Colleen's voice breaks. She sobs. Someone passes her the tissues.

"Finally, I moved. John and I are together now. His mom and dad live in the same building. John goes down with me to see them, and all she does is lie on the bed. They're still doing drugs. John was in custody twice. To get him home, I took guardianship. I don't get funding from anybody. I know she was smoking marijuana and drinking when she was pregnant. I don't know if there's anything wrong there. So it's me and John against the world right now," she says, forcing out a joyless "ha ha ha." She says, "I brought him here this morning. You could hear him screaming down the hall. But now he's settled in. It's just day by day."

She passes the phone to Tom, who gives it to his wife, Cindy. She says, "We have one grandson, our daughter's child. The father is down east. He's not in the picture. My daughter used lots of drugs and whatever since she was a teenager. She would clean up her act sometimes. When she came back from the East and had Cody, the deal between her and the father was that they'd get off drugs. Cody was a cocaine baby.

"She cleaned up her act, went back to school, got a degree and a good job. Her house ended up being a drug pit and a tattoo parlor. People were coming and going. Cody was exposed to all kinds of things, and we're not sure of all of them. He was kidnapped by a drug dealer. He has abandonment issues and severe post-traumatic stress syndrome. We had him in the TAG[1] program. He continues to see his psychologist and psychiatrist monthly. He's nine now. We go up and down like a roller coaster. We never know what's gonna trigger him. Overall, he's a pretty good student, if he can just stay focused. He's come a long way."

---

1   Trauma attachment group.

Cindy shakes her head. "Our life changed," she grimaces. A half-smile forms on her lips as she remembers. "We were retired and started to travel. That went by the wayside. But we have a passport for him. We have full guardianship. We never got any funding. We had to fight through the courts. His mother got into trouble with the law, and she's not allowed to see him for eighteen months. After that, we don't know. He's terrified to go out and play at school because he's afraid someone's gonna come and grab him."

Someone asks, "What are the effects of the cocaine?"

"When he was born," Cindy says, "he had a lot of bladder and urinary tract infections. We didn't realize why. Later they informed us, and our daughter admitted using cocaine. We've found out since then that it's not just the mother's use of cocaine but the father's. The sperm's affected. It's a lot of behavioural issues. The doctor said more would come out as he gets older. His listening ability probably. We don't know all the problems."

She hands the "stick" back to Tom. He's about to speak when a dog seems to bark. *Inside the room.* "Woof! Woof! Woof!" Luke puts his head down, and we can only see the top of his hat. He digs into his pants pocket for his phone. Tom says, "Feed that dog, eh?" Everybody laughs but Luke. He frowns and rushes into the hall.

Tom says, "When Cody came off his medication, we expected a disaster, but he hasn't been too bad." He talks about the demonstration of learning at the school. Four families came at one time, and Cody and the children got to show what they were learning.

Cindy asks for the "stick" back. She says when she took Cody for his regular blood work and EKG, the doctor discovered he has a class 1 blockage. He's on medication for anxiety and ADHD, but the cardiologist said the meds weren't safe because of his heart condition. Three days later Cindy took Cody to get running shoes before his judo class, and she said "he was throwing his shoes in the store and just going crazy." Fortunately, after class, the instructor told Cindy that Cody was focused on judo and did well in class.

Luke shuffles in from the hallway and sits back down.

Cindy says the heart condition could be related to stress. "Because his mother's been in the picture. He heard about the police looking for her and was afraid she'd show up at school." Cody's canker sores came back too, she says, and that's a sure sign of stress. But the pediatrician's happy he's off the meds, Cindy says, and she is too. The meds helped for a year and a half, but Cindy hopes he can control himself now without them. "Feedback?" she says. "Of course."

Marsha is up next. "My problem," she says, "is my son, thirty-six and addicted to alcohol. Although he's already five months going to meetings and trying to clean himself up, two weeks ago he had a breakdown for one day. I got there, and he was in my daughter's place, and just me asking why really upset him. He has an anger problem. He wasn't *drunk* drunk, but he was drinking. The next day, he didn't remember anything: that he was swearing at me, that he didn't want to see me or talk to me. I don't raise his daughter, although I have had her in my care a few times, just so she doesn't see what's going on at home. But I'm worried. I want to make sure I know what other people do and how they deal with it. That's why I'm here. Also, I am the foster mom of an eight-year-old girl. She's a cocaine baby. At my age, I could be her grandma." Marsha passes my phone to Angela.

Angela tells us that she's been raising her two grandkids pretty much since they were born. "My daughter is a drug addict. The father of the baby is abusive. He's an addict and in jail right now. I hope they deport him. Michele's been on drugs since she was twelve, and it's been one heck of a life with her. She has no mother instincts. She treats the kids like annoying siblings. So I have to be there. We all live together.

"I phoned child welfare. They came in and said they were giving me temporary custody. They told me I couldn't go to work. I wasn't allowed to leave the kids alone [with their mother] because she can be abusive. So I lost my job, and child welfare won't fund me. I don't know what to do. I tried getting on unemployment. They said they won't help me unless I look for a job. But I don't know how to go and get a job if I have no one to watch the kids, and I can't leave them. You can't drag them out to job interviews, and you can't get a subsidy for daycare unless you've got a job." Angela speaks in a calm, measured tone, as if this is happening to someone else. Then she moans: "It's overwhelming. Geoffrey just turned four and the baby just turned one. I'm overloaded. Michele is twenty-six but acts like she's thirteen. She hasn't a clue. She won't help, you know?"

"Would you like any feedback?" Julie asks. Angela shakes her head and passes the phone to Meghan.

"I'm raising two grandchildren with Jim," she says. "Daisy is eight and Joe is ten. She's my son's daughter and he's her half-brother. My son had a relationship with a young lady with addiction problems. They lived together about a year after Daisy was born, and everything fell apart. My son moved out. When Daisy was three, somebody phoned Children's Services to report problems in the home. They told the mom to find a place for the kids immediately or they'd apprehend them. So she phoned me and said, 'Can you keep them for a few days?' Their mom eventually went into rehab, came out, and promised she'd start a new life, et cetera. But it didn't work. We've had no contact with her for over four years.

"My son has struggled with addictions since junior high. He's doing well now. He showed up at Christmas, said he wanted to change his life. He's been doing all the right things. He's in recovery two months now. We have permission from social services for him to live with us. So this is a brand new thing, three adults and two kids instead of two and two. The kids have a number of issues: trauma, needing to attach to a new family, anxiety, and we think FASD. We don't really know what we're dealing with. That's our story."

Jim says, "We're actually supporting three kids, because Jerry is—what would you say?—maybe sixteen emotionally.

He's trying to learn how to be a parent to kids who are eight and ten. He has never been a parent, really. Never had that responsibility."

Meghan adds, "He hasn't really been a son or a family member since he started to mess around with drugs in school." She's not visibly upset, but she excuses herself and walks out the door, leaving her purse and coat behind.

Jim says Jerry is new to rehab and wants the kids to come live with him. Jim says Children's Services thinks he can become the kids' sole parent in just two months, which would be a "recipe for certain failure."

Jim says he's concerned about Meghan's health; she's not been well since Jerry came to live with them three months ago: can't sleep, upset stomach—that kind of thing. Having Jerry in rehab is the answer to her prayers, but this transition time is stressful. But it's great to have a live-in babysitter. He and Meghan have gone to movies, restaurants—they've felt freer than they have for five years. But there's serious disagreement about Daisy's ADHD medication. Jerry is totally opposed to the drugs, and a new social worker takes his side, against Jim and Meghan and the psychiatrist they've been working with for two years. "This social worker horns in, doesn't know shit about us or the kids, never met the kids," Jim says. "The guy talked down to us like we were idiots." Jim looks around the room. Most are nodding in agreement. They've had workers like that too.

"The next big thing is scheduled for a month from now," he says. "A talking circle run by an Aboriginal

Elder. It'll involve us, Jerry, social workers, and anybody else we want for support." Julie makes a sweeping motion with her hands, pointing to the circle. "Here you go," she says.

"Yeah!" Jim says. "Maybe we should invite all of you!" Everybody laughs. "Or we should just have that group come here."

Julie asks Jim if he'd like feedback, and he says, "Of course," as Meghan comes back in and sits next to him.

Now the check-in is over, Julie goes back to April and Luke for the feedback round. Luke says the phone call was the neighbour asking to be picked up at the hospital. He feels obligated but wonders how he and April can manage.

April clenches her fists and moans, "I don't know what's going to happen."

Somebody else in the circle is clear and firm, though. "Do not pick him up!" she says. "No, honestly, if he has nowhere to go, they have to put him somewhere. Once you get him, they'll wash their hands. I know."

Julie adds, "He's not your responsibility."

Vicky says, "I'd have trouble helping somebody like that."

Julie asks if they've phoned Children's Services. They haven't. Julie says, "Even looking after the children— they're not your responsibility. Eric is. And having two extra kids is affecting Eric. And your health!"

"We have to be careful," Vicky adds. "We're the people who have taken in our grandkids, and we'd probably gladly take in anybody else if we could. That's the way we are. But there are limits."

Everybody has an opinion: where to draw boundaries, methods of self-care, who to call for help, who's responsible for whom, et cetera. Julie suggests that April and Luke phone the mental health line to get the neighbour some help. Anne, the second social worker, says, "And call the social worker. But *don't* pick him up!"

April's still not sure. Anne tells her to think about this in a different way: the neighbour did the best he could; help him get help, instead of Band-Aiding it. Otherwise his kids will continue to suffer.

April and Luke look at each other but don't say anything. They know they have a hard decision to make. Julie asks, "All right if we move on?" They nod.

"Okay. Greg. Tom's basketball overnight party."

Vicky says, "I wouldn't go that far. Tom says, 'I *have to* hang out with the guys. You *have to* trust me.' I say, 'Why can't you just come home? Aren't you gonna be able to drive?' " Julie and Vicky picture Tom at a party with ten other teenagers and alcohol. Vicky says he's "never given us grief." She shrugs. "I guess he may have to hang himself once or twice before he finds out. Besides, the coaches will be there, and the party is at a parent's home." She whispers, "I hope he has a really good time." Julie says, "Do you really? You sound like you kind of don't." Everybody laughs, including Greg, who has been listening quietly.

Vicky says she wants Tom to come home instead of spending the night. It's Greg's idea to drop him off and let him spend the night. Some people think it's less risky if Tom doesn't take a vehicle to the party; some say they should trust him, since he's been a good kid so far.

From the other side of the circle, somebody says, "A friend of mine lost her virginity *at a Bible camp!*" Somebody asks if they think drugs will be involved. Anne says, "They're gonna try it at some point."

Vicky wonders about the worst that could happen: Tom goes to the party, spends the night, and they get a call from the police or the hospital. Anne interrupts: "How are you ever gonna know you can trust him? What needs to happen?"

"His actions," Vicky answers. "He has to have a chance to prove himself." Anne smiles and says, "Yeah. By controlling all he can and can't have, you'd limit all the great work you two have done to this point. Your ultimate goal has always been to launch." Greg smiles.

Julie asks if anybody has anything to add. Vicky says, "If you need anybody to clean your closets, call Nancy!" Everybody laughs.

Julie turns to Mary. "Okay. Eyebrow stitches." Vicky asks if she did a report. Mary says that a while ago their social worker saw Nancy with a cast on her ankle and was upset he wasn't told. They had to do a report afterwards, including a statement by someone else who was there; they were lucky that a police officer witnessed the event and was able to help out.

Mary says she didn't realize there should be a report, but since Nick got cut at school, she thinks finding witnesses should be simple.

"The work on practising gratitude sounds good," Julie says. "How's it working? Are you doing something in the morning? At supper?"

"If you're being crazy because of something," Mary says, "what can you be grateful for? What about your breakfast this morning? 'Cause there's kids who don't get breakfast. Or that you have a bed to sleep in. Just be grateful for the things you have. Gratitude is good for us all to practise."

Cindy agrees: "Cody has to compliment somebody every day at school. He has a real problem talking with people. I noticed at soccer when they got the gold medals out, he was the only one who didn't clap. For anybody."

Somebody says, "They need to express their feelings. Their feelings need to be validated."

Mary says, "There are times they're upset about something. You listen to that. Instead of complaining they don't have this toy, I encourage them to look at all the toys they do have."

"We're talking about two different things," Anne says. "Timing of gratitude is important. When he wants another toy, you're helping him reframe the situation. It's not so much about being grateful. Reframing is a powerful tool. It can get us out of situations we can't change. And feelings are important. If we're angry and upset and can't verbalize it and can't validate it, it's going to come out in our behaviour." She says, "I like the gratitude. I think it's a great way to start or end the day. Grateful for a delicious supper or that soccer is over for a while. *Grateful for driving home with the sun in my eyes!*"

Somebody says, "You're blinded and hit the ditch, and you're grateful for that?" Everybody laughs.

Julie asks if anyone has feedback for Cindy and Tom. Cindy interrupts: "We're back to the high-pitched squealing. It drives you crazy!" Someone asks if it's because of ending Cody's meds, and Cindy says no, he's been doing it since he talked to his dad on the phone a couple of weeks ago. But he's been getting worse. "I can't handle it. He does it until I lose my cool and yell at him to stop. I have to shout, '*Please stop doing it!*' He does it all the time, especially in the car going to school. It's such a high pitch, you know. Like a two-year-old."

Anne asks if it's the physical or the emotional part of it that bothers her, and Cindy says, "It breaks your ear drums! It hurts! And he keeps doing it until I yell at him. He even did it in the shoe store yesterday. Here's this nine-year-old who looks eleven, and he's doing a high-pitched, two-year-old squeal!"

Julie suggests maybe she could give him some silly putty to put in his pocket to play with; instead of yelling at Cody, Cindy could just say, "Where's your silly putty?"

Anne wonders if having bubble wrap would help. He could pop bubbles instead of screaming.

Someone says there must be a reason. "I think he does it to annoy me," Cindy says.

Anne wonders if the primary concern is Cindy's reaction, or is something going on in Cody. Cindy says, "He says he likes it. He told me he likes to annoy people and see their reaction." Anne says, "That puts him in charge and makes him the bad guy. It could be his way to get control of himself. Because his life is out of control. He's self-stimulating, self-regulating, if he's trying to control his feelings. Maybe you could try music? It could be music he puts on and turns off. His music. But you said it's happened since that phone call?"

"Yes," Cindy says. "First the thumb-sucking and now the squealing. Maybe he's regressing. The thumb-sucking was the baby, and now it's a two-year-old. That's where he is a lot right now."

"That's sad," Anne says. "Let's put ourselves in his shoes: a nine-year-old boy who had contact with his dad and then suddenly no more. Thank God his dad didn't phone back! What can you do to support Cody to get back to being Cody? You guys were making incredible gains with those behaviours. Out of all this, what did you guys learn about contact with the dad?"

Cindy says that ever since he first had problems with his mother phoning the house, they trained Cody never to answer the phone. They're confident they can intercept calls from Cody's dad before they get to Cody.

"Do you take stuff like this to the therapist?" Julie asks. "I assume you still go to a therapist." Cindy says they do, but Cody wasn't co-operative the last time they went.

The clock in the room strikes twelve. Mary and several others get up to leave. Julie says, "People can stay if they want. I know some other people wanted feedback. It's just those who have kids in the daycare." A few say goodbye and chat briefly on their way out.

Once the room is quiet again, Anne goes back to Cody's squealing. "I think you should just try something. The music. The ball. See if it makes a change." She says if Cody were her child, she'd make a plan, decide beforehand what to do the next time he squeals. Cindy wonders if she should pull the car off onto the shoulder and get him to squeal outside. Anne suggests that maybe Cindy should get out of the car and let Cody yell in the car; then he won't be tempted to run away.

Luke mumbles, "Maybe parrot the kid." "I had a parent do that," Anne adds. Cindy shakes her head. "My throat won't take what his does," she says.

Vicky says, "I stopped at a gas station and just got out. I'd had enough. We had driven all the way to Vancouver. Twelve, thirteen years old! Don't wait until then."

Mary comes back in with her 3-year-old, and he says hello to everyone. He giggles, smiles, hugs Anne, and waves goodbye. The other grandparents wave and say, "Bye-bye!"

By now, the rest of the grandparents are standing up and putting on their coats.

Anne wishes everybody a happy Easter and reminds them there won't be meetings for the next two weeks; the next one, she says, will be in a new building a few blocks away. Everyone wishes Anne and Julie happy Easter as they walk out the door.

In the hallway, Mary puts coats and boots on her three preschoolers. Others chat nearby in groups of two or three. They know they have more in common with the people in this group than with their other friends. They want to extend this social outing, because for most of them, this is a rare opportunity to enjoy the company of other adults, kid-free.

As I drive back into the city, I remember that for most of us the very existence of the group was a surprise. We were so busy getting ourselves and our grandkids through each day that we didn't have time or energy to look for other people who did the same thing. People who raise grandkids often feel like prisoners of their circumstances, without a social circle.

For some, their own relatives cut off contact. Friends tell them they were "absolutely stupid" to try to raise a grandchild, that they "couldn't believe you would even consider doing this." People laughed at one step-grandfather because "they aren't even your grandchildren!" The grandparents in this support group talked about how they feel they "don't fit into society anymore," how they're not accepted in social circles of people their age. The parents of their grandchildren's classmates, meanwhile, are in their twenties and thirties and don't want to socialize with people who are as old as their parents.

One grandmother told me, "I don't know where I'd be if it wasn't for this group. I felt so alone before, almost embarrassed because it felt like, 'Can't you raise these kids? Why are you messing up all the time? *Don't you know anything?*'" Another said, "I didn't talk about my feelings. I've been able to talk about my feelings here without being judged." A grandfather said, "This group has been a really good way to reconnect with the 'grandparent condition.' It's been valuable to be with people who are in the same boat." Another said it was like a date: he and his wife get out and socialize with adults their own age. His wife said, "other people have no concept of what we're going through. This group helped us pull through a lot of bad times. It's given us an outlet where we can talk and be ourselves, and people understand."

Grandparent groups like this are hard to find, and besides, grandparents who are busy raising little children usually don't have time to go to meetings, even if these groups offer exactly the kind of self-care they need. Foster parents, on the other hand, have formal associations all across Canada, with well-established support networks and training programs. In Alberta, kinship caregivers are invited to foster conferences and training sessions; grandparents like us, we're a small minority on the fringes. And though the two groups are very different, even social workers have difficulty seeing the differences. Linda Krauskopf, on the other hand, is an expert who lives in both groups. She's been a foster parent for twenty-eight years, and her 2-year-old grandson was living with her when we spoke.

FOUR

Foster Care:
Parenting by the Dozen

*In unity there is strength. We can move
mountains when we're united and enjoy
life. Without unity we are victims.*

—*Bill Bailey*

Linda already had eight kids in her home and wasn't expecting a baby. When the baby came, at 2:00 a.m., she had no crib to put her in. So she put her on a sectional chesterfield and placed pillows around it so she'd be safe.

"My husband gets up in the morning," Linda said, "and he hears this 'hmmm, hmmm,' and he says, 'Did we get a cat?' Because our house was full of animals. He says, 'Omigod! The foster kids have brought another animal home!' He goes in the corner, and there's a baby! He says, 'Where did that come from?' He'd slept through the whole thing!" Linda laughed and said, "So we ended up adopting that one." She seemed oddly casual telling me about it, as if this kind of thing was a part of her daily routine, like brushing her teeth: another day, another kid adopted. Then she explained that in twenty-eight years of foster parenting, she's only—*only*—had sixty kids, and she's adopted just one of them. That was this 4-month-old, who she calls her "sectional baby," and who increased the kid population in Linda's house to nine.

When I met Linda Krauskopf, she was ready to retire from foster parenting. Her husband, who never had biological children of his own and who agreed to foster parent so he could experience the joy of parenting children, had just died of cancer. When we spoke, Linda had two teenage foster daughters still in her care. Her own 2-year-old grandson and his mother lived with her at the time, so she was a grandparenting parent too.

Most people need grief counseling and maybe time away to get through the loss of a spouse, but Linda preferred to keep working. When we talked, she served as the Edmonton regional director for the Alberta Foster Parents Association, represented Alberta as part of a national foster care working group, and ran a secondhand store that hired people who were recovering from addictions or had mental illnesses. She's an extrovert who gets energy from working with others. She's an activist who works with associations and governments to make things right for kids, and she doesn't mind crossing swords with politicians and bureaucrats when she has to. Despite having just lost her husband, Linda seemed to have two or three times the energy I had.

Linda thrives on work and chaos. That's how she grew up, and that's why she was so good at foster parenting. Recalling her dad, she said that "anybody down on their luck, he was there to help out. He had a handicapped friend he went to school with. He'd check up on him to make sure he was okay. When one of my brother's friends was going through a bad situation, my dad said, 'You don't need to live there; come stay with us.' " Linda said, "You never knew who was going to be at the house. You never knew where my dad was. He'd pick somebody up from jail because they'd done something stupid. He'd go bail 'em out because nobody else would."

For Linda, as with all the best foster parents, her work is much more than a job. One big difference between kinship caregiving and foster parenting is that some people do get into fostering for the money, even though the rates are designed only to cover expenses. That's why the money isn't taxable.

The rates in Alberta range from $783 to $1,978 per month per child; the more high-needs the child is, the higher the rate and the more training required. Foster parents must have training to get into fostering, and they have to continue training every year. For skipped-generation grandparents, though, training is either optional or non-existent, and since 2014, grandparents in the Kinship Care program get only the base rate, between $783 and $1,154 per month. They are not eligible to receive the "skill fees" that foster parents get, which are based on the child's needs and the caregiver's training.[1] No grandparent I know of raises a grandchild because of the money. In fact, the money usually covers only about half the basic expenses.

Linda says the money she gets is for the kids, not her. "My husband's parents were foster parents for years and were still fostering when I came into the picture," she said. Her husband's best friends were foster parents too. Linda had two children of her own from a previous marriage. When she remarried, she and her husband wanted to have children, but she'd had a hysterectomy. So, she said, "we just rolled into" fostering.

She told me the area north of Edmonton where she lives is "the breadbasket of fostering." She said Sturgeon County used to have more foster homes than the whole city of Edmonton. The culture is different there. Wives are more likely to stay at home, it's cheaper to live there than in the city, and most jobs require a commute.

When they started fostering, she and her husband each had small vehicles, big enough only for the four in their family. Because this was a new commitment for them, they decided to get a van and prepare their home for more children, unlike grandparents who get a call from a social worker saying, "We've apprehended your grand-children because where they were living isn't safe." The

---

1   The rates vary across Canada. The rate in Ontario is only $280 per child, and that is at the mercy of the regional managers of the system. Some grandparents get nothing.

grandparents have to make a profoundly life-changing decision with very little time to think about it, much less time to get new furniture or a bigger car.

Grandparents typically create emergency accommodation for their unexpected grandchildren—sleeping bags on floors, sheets and blankets on chesterfields—and then battle government agencies to help them pay for dressers, bunk beds, car seats, clothing, toothbrushes, and other necessities. Or they simply pay for it out of their own pockets, even if that means drawing down their pension savings or taking on a new job. In the case of Linda and her husband, however, and foster parents more generally, Children's Services pays set amounts for each child, depending on the child's needs. Another crucial difference is that foster parents don't have to face, every single day, the shame and grief grandparents do because their own child has failed as a parent. They don't live in the isolation that such shame and grief brings in its wake. They don't have the deep personal connection with the parents of their foster children that keeps them up at night worrying whether those parents are freezing to death outside or working the streets or overdosing on crystal meth or fentanyl.

Grandparents can access self-help groups, like the one we saw in the last chapter. And of course, they can start a group themselves, but few have time or energy for that. Foster parents know from the beginning that they have the Alberta Foster Parents Association, or a similar group, to tell them what the rates of pay are, what their rights are, what programs are available to help them, who to appeal to for help, and the like.

I was in a kincare group where we heard social workers had pressured a grandmother to adopt a grandchild. The grandmother didn't know the financial impact that would have on her, nor what her options were. She was shocked to hear she'd be giving up thousands of dollars of kincare support if she adopted. She was dismayed to learn that the social worker's promises to cover dental care and prescription drugs, for example, are only for one year on a renewable contract, even though her responsibility is permanent. I've heard many stories of social workers threatening to take grandchildren away and send them into foster care, or to give them to fictitious people waiting in line to adopt them. An isolated grandmother wouldn't know that's a bluff unless she talked to somebody who'd been through the same experience.

I know grandparents who were lied to by a social worker for six years. They were told repeatedly that kincare people don't get any funding for respite, even though respite is a standard practice for foster parents. That worker was apparently more interested in saving a few dollars than giving the couple the occasional breaks she knew they needed to maintain the high quality of parenting to which they were committed. If they'd been members of a foster parent association or had access to a grandparenting group, they would have known better.

Linda told me that thanks to the Foster Parents Association, the system is changing. She said the plan is for kincare parents to get training from the beginning. That way, kincare parents will know their rights and the range of support they're entitled to. That way, grandparents will no longer be at the mercy of social workers. The training probably cannot be mandatory, she said, but if it's tailored to the unique needs of kincare caregivers and sold the right way, it will be a big help to them and their children.

"We have a lot of Native homes," Linda said, "and we have to look at them differently.…We have a lot of Native families, older families, grandparents who maybe don't speak or read English or are uneducated." Grandparents take great pride in their parenting ability, she said, and may well be offended when social workers try to tell them what to do: "I'm the grandparent, and you're going to tell me how to grandparent my child?" The Foster Parents Association isn't part of an impersonal government bureaucracy, she said, and it's in a better position to break through these barriers.

The typical grandmother has wisdom based on her experience, but she may not know how to help a child with special needs, and she doesn't know that she doesn't know. Most grandmothers wouldn't know the science around attachment disorder or post-traumatic stress disorder, wouldn't know the recent discoveries about fetal alcohol syndrome, and probably wouldn't know how to deal with mental illness or the dynamics of addiction.[2]

---

2 When my own children were born, between 1977 and 1983, little if anything was known about what happened to the fetus when the mother consumed…*(continued)*

Kincare parents living in poverty tend to be more defensive about receiving outside help than middle-class parents are, Linda said. "If you tell them there's this program called Kinship Care and you could get some money for that child to go to hockey, and you could go on a vacation with some of the money if you wanted to, and you can get some money during the month," Linda said, "the only thing you can do is tell them. Some people will be very offended." Grandparents may not have even heard the term "kinship care" because it has only been in common use for ten to fifteen years.

Kinship Care became a government program in North America and Europe because research showed it was better for children to be with people they know than with strangers. Children apparently can do better with a family they know, even a dysfunctional one, than in a happy, healthy home full of strangers, as long as the family is relatively safe. Part of that is the uncertainty, the children not knowing whether they'll be moved from foster home to foster home; if Children's Services commits to keeping children with family, they have at least some stability.

Some children have access to both foster care and Kinship Care. Linda told me about three of her foster children. Two had been living with their grandparents,

---

...alcohol. This was about the same time alcohol manufacturers started opening up the hitherto untapped female market for their product. In North American and elsewhere during the first half of the twentieth century, it was culturally unacceptable for respectable middle-class women to drink more than, say, a glass of wine. An excellent book on the subject is *Drink: The Intimate Relationship between Women and Alcohol*, by Ann Dowsett Johnston (Toronto: Harper Collins, 2013).

but then the grandfather got cancer. The grandmother couldn't support him and look after the kids too. "She put them into care because there was nobody else," Linda said. This lasted for about six months before the children's mother got pregnant again. Everyone hoped she was changing her life and would be able to care for her own children. And she did get the children for about six months, but then there were more problems, and Linda had to take them back. One of them was that "sectional baby" she took in in the middle of the night.

The mother of these three children had three others too. Despite the efforts of the grandmother, aunts, and others, the children could not stay together, and they were adopted by different families. Linda told me she helped one of the girls later in life find one of her sisters, but they never did find a brother because Children's Services wouldn't give them the information they needed to track him down. Privacy laws in that case prevented family from reconnecting, even after the children had grown up.

Linda said she always encouraged her foster children to talk about their birth parents because it's important to stay connected with the story of their early lives, especially if it's impossible to be with their biological families. The mother of four of Linda's foster children was a homeless person in inner-city Edmonton, she said. Linda encouraged the children to go to the Boyle Street Centre and meet her there. "That's their mom," she said, "but I'm the real mom. They'll talk to her. They'll show up there with basic needs: shampoo, soap, deodorant, and underwear for her. They'll drop it off and see her."

So, who *is* the real mom? Is a grandmother more of a mom than a foster mother? Which is the better way to raise children when the parents can't or won't: kincare or foster care? Linda's experience shows that the system needs both, but even some foster parents don't understand the dynamics of kincare. A friend of mine and his wife have fostered dozens of children. I told him about a grandmother who gave up her retirement, her freedom, her social life, all the opportunities open to her as a senior citizen, in order to take in two grandchildren. He was offended. He was appalled that this woman, without training and on the spur of the moment, would think she could do a better job with her grandkids than people like him and his wife could as foster parents.

I said, "If these were your grandchildren and you knew—as you do—that a lot of foster parents aren't as good at it as you are, and since you also know how much it damages kids to be bounced from place to place and the likelihood of that happening, would you let your own grandchildren go into foster care? Or would you take them in yourself? Think about it. Your own grandchildren cared for by strangers in a system where you know tragedies occur, where things happen, sometimes not because the foster parents aren't good enough but because other foster kids in the same home could become violent or lead the kids into drugs or crime?" He thought about it and shook his head. "I guess you're right. When you put it that way."

Whether kids go to foster homes, kincare homes, or both, they suffer profound damage, a physical brain injury in fact, because the people whose lives they were born into—their biological parents—are no longer with them. Both foster parents and kincare parents have to deal with the consequences of that broken first attachment.

If their biological parents abused them with drugs or alcohol in utero, if they neglected them or traumatized them through poverty or sexual or physical assault, if the parents died in a war zone, a refugee camp, a car accident, or a cardiac ward, that all factors into the children's healing process. Separating a child from his or her birth parents is itself a traumatic event that literally changes the child's brain chemistry and cellular structure (as we'll see in the next chapter). Both foster parents and kincare parents have to learn what each child needs, and to respond in loving ways, with all their hearts, even though love alone is never enough. Both can learn to become their children's day-to-day therapists. The biggest difference is that grandparents always hold the biological parent—their son or daughter—close to the heart that that child of theirs broke when they left their own children behind. You might say that these parents of a missing generation, as it were, carry in their own hearts and brains the scars of damaged attachment.

FIVE

Healing from Broken Attachments

If you lived inside my head, you'd be scared too.
—Seven-year-old participant
in the TAG program

Consider the following two scenarios, both based on real children's experiences.

Five-year-old Suzy gets up at 7:00 a.m. when Skippy, her pet beagle, jumps up on her bed and licks her face. Suzy's mother, Betty, comes into the room, sees Suzy and Skippy in bed. Betty smiles, and a lilting soprano voice says, "Good morning, Suzy! Did you have a good sleep?" Suzy says, "I dreamt I was at gramma and grampa's farm chasing a frog in the grass and Skippy ran over to lick my face. And here he is! And you are too!" Betty kisses Suzy and helps her pick out her clothes for kindergarten. Then they both go to the kitchen, where Suzy's dad, Tom, has breakfast on the table: hot pancakes drowning in maple syrup, golden sausage links on the side, the smell of smoked pork in the air. Betty and Suzy greet Tom with hugs and kisses.

In another house, 6-year-old Jeremy wakes up at 9:00 a.m., groggy after a restless night. His parents were downstairs with friends drinking, yelling, playing loud heavy-metal music, and slamming doors until two in the morning. They sent Jeremy to his room at nine, when the party started, and he lay in bed listening. He held Max, his stuffed gorilla, tight against his chest. He dozed off many times. He woke up in a panic when a door slammed, again when a beer bottle smashed against a wall, and again when people yelled cusswords so loudly he could hear them clearly through the pillows he'd put over his ears. The stereo's woofer shook the walls, the floor, the bed, Jeremy's skull. The noises were familiar, normal, even comforting, like the smell of vomit on Max and the stale sweat and urine on unwashed clothes scattered around his room. This morning, the sun shines brightly in the window. Jeremy is hungry. He goes downstairs and sees his mother and father curled up on the rug under a sleeping bag. He finds a bag with a few Cheezies in it and stuffs a handful into his mouth.

Every family has a culture. For most parents, the rules in their home are like the rules where they grew up, modified to suit their own circumstances. These rules are usually unwritten: kids set the table for supper, brush their teeth morning and night, make their beds before breakfast, say please and thank you, et cetera. The hope is that kids imitate the parents' behaviour, like ducklings walking in a row behind their mother.

One of the first lessons Dr. Andrew Bremness teaches the parents in his traumatic attachment group (TAG)[1] is that we're all raising kids who have been separated from their biological parents. That separation alone, he says, is enough to cause symptoms of post-traumatic stress disorder. He says that when these kids come into our homes, they bring in their bones, in fact in all the cells of their body, the culture they absorbed very early on, beginning in the womb. Maybe they were in a war zone in Ethiopia or a drug house in Edmonton. They were probably abused or neglected. He says it's as if these kids used to live by rugby rules, and in our house we play soccer. Imagine a player running onto a soccer pitch, grabbing the ball in her hands, and running at the opposing goalie. Or a hockey player, skates and all, standing in the batter's box on a baseball diamond swinging a hockey stick.

If Suzy and Jeremy switched places, they'd have to learn new rules. But the first rules they learned were hard-wired into their brains since conception.[2] Jeremy would still be

---

1 TAG is a program of CASA: Child, Adolescent and Family Services, a nonprofit agency that provides child, adolescent, and family mental health services in central and northern Alberta. Attachment programs operate throughout North America, but Edmonton's TAG program is unique in that it utilizes group dynamics in addition to individual therapy.

2 "Hard-wired," is a metaphor. The neural strands in our brains form circuits like wires in a computer, but they're not wires. Recent brain research confirms that neural plasticity, the brain's ability to change itself, enables a person to develop new neural circuits and to override the old ones that resulted, for example, from trauma.

on hyper-alert if he moved into Suzy's home and suddenly had clean sheets and silence at night and attentive parents in the morning; Suzy would be in shock, overwhelmed by the noise, the smells, the lack of attention in Jeremy's home. Every caregiver in TAG faces a challenge like this. The objective for the program's two years and beyond is to give us tools to become our kids' live-in therapists, and to develop new circuits in our kids' brains. We each come to TAG with our own culture and history, and TAG gives us basic training in brain science, attachment theory, and how to manage our own emotional baggage. For grand-parents over sixty with a generation missing between us and the kids, there's plenty of baggage.

The principal tool is "kit time," which aims to establish a new primary attachment between each child and one "parent."[3] Kit time mimics the attachment of a nursing mother and her newborn: intimate, one-on-one attention. TAG kids may not have been nursed as newborns, but they all lived in a womb for many months, and their primary attachment to their biological parents has been broken. The point is to give them a healthy attachment now as 7- or 8-year-olds.

Kit time is essentially playtime, in whatever form that might take to match the child's chronological and emo-tional ages. And yet TAG's guidelines are pretty strict. If there are two caregivers, only one does regular kit time.

---

3   No TAG child comes with biological parents, of course. TAG staff call us
    "parents" because that is our role. I am my child's grandfather, but as the male
    role model in the house, I am also his father, and his grandmother is his mother.

Kit time should be at least twenty minutes every day. Caregivers get a suggested shopping list: paper, pencils, paints and brushes, crayons and markers, playdough or Plasticine, scissors, glue stick, puppets, a family of dolls, hand lotion, a special bar of soap with a scent the child chooses, walkie-talkies, stickers, balloons, a small blanket, storybooks, a journal, games, playing cards, et cetera.[4] It's important that parent and child shop together and that the child select things he or she wants to play with, including things not on the list and things they may already have. Everything then goes into a portable container. That full container is "the kit."

Until the 1950s—back when I was a child—attachment theory wasn't even heard of. Everyone, including psychiatrists, thought children were so resilient they could be separated from their parents without harm. Or they thought children should be "seen and not heard." In those days, hospitals kept sick children apart from their parents for days, or even weeks if they needed major surgery. Dr. John Bowlby and two of his students studied the lasting emotional impact of these separations, and they changed the pediatric hospital practices dramatically when they proved the separations were harmful. Now, the parents' presence is a valued part of the healing process. In those days, psychiatrists and psychologists were just learning about post-traumatic stress for combat veterans, but now, thanks to pioneers like Bowlby and Dr. Bruce Perry, the

---

4   List courtesy of CASA.

medical profession recognizes that breaking childhood attachment has an impact as profound and long-lasting as what used to be called "shell shock."[5]

Most of the TAG sessions during the first four months include twenty minutes of kit time for the whole group of about ten kids and ten parents. They gather on mats in a room with a one-way mirror on one wall. Staff observe the interactions and make notes. These and other notes help parents and staff understand their progress and enable them to make the necessary adjustments. Every week, before kit time, while other staff have structured playtime with the kids, Dr. Bremness spends an hour or so teaching parents about brain development and attachment theory, and he invites parents to discuss their experiences over the last week.

He asks, "Who has something that's happened this week that they really need to share with the group?"[6] Alicia, an aunt-caregiver, says, "Trish and I were driving down Whyte Avenue last Friday. She was mad. I wouldn't let her spend the evening with her brother. When we got to the red light, she just opened the door and ran down the sidewalk! By the time I found a place to park, I didn't know where she was or where to look. It took me half an hour to find her!"

---

5 Perry's *The Boy Who Was Raised as a Dog and Other Stories from a Child Psychiatrist's Notebook* (New York: Basic Books, 2008) contains several dramatic case studies that illustrate the profound impact of broken and unhealthy attachment.

6 I've created this discussion from personal observations and modified it to ensure confidentiality. All names have been changed.

Dr. Bremness says, "You told me Trish just had a call from her mother a day or two before that. Do you think this could have been a reaction to that? When a bio parent suddenly comes back into the picture, we can expect problems. Trish is getting pulled back to the unsafe place she came from. It's a place she's familiar with and finds attractive for that reason. But it's the place she learned those 'rugby rules.' " He looks around the room and asks, "Does this sound familiar to anybody else?"

He waits in silence for maybe half a minute. Natalie coughs. Everybody looks at her and waits for her to say something. Natalie has had this cough for years. Her doctor can't find a cause. But Natalie knows it's stress, the constant worry: "Is my daughter dead? Is she sleeping in the river valley, homeless, exposed to -30 degree temperatures at night?" Natalie hasn't heard from her daughter in two months and hasn't had an unmedicated eight-hour sleep for a decade. She's raising the 7-year-old grandson her own daughter couldn't.

Another grandmother in the group, Olive, realizes Natalie isn't going to speak, so she says, "Andy was playing hockey on Saturday. His mom showed up in the bleachers. He hadn't seen her for six months, not since we got the EPO.[7] She's not allowed near him, but the order doesn't work if he's in a public place." Olive rubs a spot on the back of her hand. "When I got him home after the game, he was shaking and he clung to me. A lot more than usual.

---

7   Emergency protection order.

When I put him to bed, he sobbed and wouldn't settle down unless I laid down beside him. Even then it took about an hour for him to go to sleep."

Another parent says he got a voice message from his child's biological father, who wants to see the child, even though there's been no contact for three years. Dr. Bremness says, "For TAG to work, you have to keep the bio parents away for now. We are willing to testify in court, if it comes to that. It's essential that until we've established a strong bond with you, the present parents, and the children, the bio parents need to be out of the picture. Our experience is that the process takes at least a year."

He points to Catherine, who is nursing her month-old baby girl. "Catherine's connection with little Adriana is the model for what we are all working on with our 8- and 9- and 10- and 12-year-old children. Olive, when you were lying in bed with Andy, how old would you say he was emotionally?" Olive pauses to think and says, "Probably four or six months. He couldn't talk. He was just scared."

"He was triggered back to an unsafe place," Dr. Bremness says, "when his mother could have been with an abusive boyfriend and didn't comfort Andy when he got scared. He carries that around in his body. When you do your kit time, you're reaching back into his past, back to when he was as young as Adriana, and you're rewiring his brain. You're getting into the sensorimotor part of the brain, the preverbal area at the base of the brain, where those old feelings and memories live, and you're establishing new connections. You're laying down new neural pathways to replace those old ones. You do it by playing, holding, reading to connect him to you as profoundly as Catherine and Adriana are connecting right now."

Even though previous attachments were harmful, they had some good in them, he says. The previous attachment will always be part of the child's story, and it's important to honour that by emphasizing the positive—that your mom loved you and did the best she could. He tells the group, "The science says honouring previous attachments is key to establishing the new attachment. We need to honour the bio parents' efforts and the child's efforts to establish that first attachment. If we don't get this right, the kids will turn back to the 'dark side' as teenagers. This happens when they haven't resolved loyalty issues with their birth parents. Every child needs to know and be able to say, 'I can love everybody I'm attached to. I don't have to choose.' "

When the kids come into the adults' room for kit time, each child picks a different thing to do. One parent-child pair plays Old Maid. Another plays checkers. One uncle reads his niece a story and then massages her forehead with lavender oil, her mother's favourite fragrance. A grandmother sketches a violin on a pad of paper while her child, pretending to be an art teacher, coaches grandma on how to draw the chin rest and then selects the right shade of purple for the violin's body. A foster mother rolls a set of dice that have words on them, and she and her son take turns making up a story using the words that come up.

When TAG 1 ends in April, everyone receives a diploma to honour their work so far. But the kids' excitement is mingled with sadness because they won't be coming to play with their new TAG friends for a long time, not until September. The parents worry too: "Who do I talk to when Andy throws a screaming fit at the dinner table?" "What do I do when Joanie wets the bed again?" "When Jerry's teacher phones to tell me he's been in another fight, I'm supposed to get out the kit and play with him? Sometimes I don't feel safe in the same house with him! He whacked my head with a book last week!"

At the last parents-only session in the spring, staff remind parents that when they get angry at their child, take a timeout and set that anger aside; treat the child as you would a newborn. It might seem that you're rewarding bad behaviour, but remember, the behaviour isn't the child's fault. The child is injured and needs love and support. The staff tell parents that kit time is more important and better than any drug: the relationship building, the bonding, the attachment that's happening will heal both child and caregiver/parent.

They recommend two principles for the summer break: reflective listening and sensorimotor stimulation. Reflective listening means you notice your child is mad/sad/scared, and you help the child manage the feeling: "Suzy, I can tell you're angry about something. I get angry sometimes too. When I get angry, I take a walk and look around at the trees, the sky, the snow. Sometimes I write in my journal about it. Or I just get out pencil and paper and doodle."

Acknowledge and name the emotions, they say. Sometimes that's enough. Suggest or model suitable responses. Maybe the child simply needs time alone. Sensorimotor stimulation means things like rubbing on hand cream, tickling with a feather, buying a favourite flavour of chewing gum, adding scented oil to bathwater, burning sage or incense.

TAG 2 begins at the end of August. Most of the sessions bring all the parents and children together in a large room. TAG 2's goal is to help the children discover the place where they are profoundly safe: their present family home. Every session starts with brain gym exercises led in a playful way, and some sessions include bouncing on large balls, spending time on a vibrating mattress, or in a small tent just big enough for two. These exercises stimulate the senses and awaken connections in the brain. But the primary activities in TAG 2 sessions are the sand trays and the CASA train visualization.

The CASA train starts with everybody in a circle again, lying down on body-length rubber mats.[8] The leader encourages everyone to get comfortable. He suggests parents cuddle with their child. "I invite you to close your eyes and breathe gently, in and out. Every time you breathe, relax a little more. The secret is not to try. Just let go." He asks everyone to relax their tummies, stretch out their legs, bend their ankles, wiggle their toes.

---

8   The CASA train visualization happens six or more times, and each time it progresses a little farther into the journey toward a dark cabin. The scene depicted here is what a participant would experience at the end of TAG 2, after they've gone on the imaginary trip many times, struggling with varying degrees of fear, shame, and sadness along the way.

"In the next little while," he says, "as you focus on my voice, together we will journey to a safe place. Imagine you are walking out of this room. You come to a train platform. You hear a train coming in the distance. It comes closer and closer, slows down, and stops right in front of you."

He says everyone has his or her own train car, made just for them, exactly how they like it. It's a beautiful, safe place, just for you! Wow! It can be as big or as small as you want it to be, and you can take with you anything you want. He invites everyone to look around, take in the scenery outside the window, feel the rhythm of the train as it chugs out of the station, hear the clatter of the wheels on the rail, listen to whatever music is playing.

After a while, the train arrives at a beautiful meadow. The sun is shining bright and warm. Everybody gets out. A picnic supper is spread out on a table, all the food anybody could want. There's laughter and games to play, and everybody feels safe and happy.

Off in the distance, dark clouds are forming. There's a forest some distance away from the meadow and a run-down, dark cabin in the shadows of the trees. You wonder if anybody lives there. You notice a path leading to the cabin. You take your parent's hand and walk up to it. There's a faint light in the window. You slowly walk up and peek inside. You see a small child. The child looks a little like you. But this child is cold, hungry, and alone. You pull some food out of your backpack, as well as a teddy bear and a blanket. You offer them to the child. You say some kind words to the child. The child smiles back.

You notice a family in the cabin with the child. They look unhappy. You walk up to the door, still holding your parent's hand, and you knock. The family lets you in. What do you see? What would you like to say to the family? What do they say to you?

The child you saw in the window takes your hand, and you both go outside. You look at each other and smile. You invite the child to come with you back to the meadow, back to the train. You board the train and get back into the comfort of your own train car. You settle into your safe place on the train. You know this is your own safe place, a place you can come to anytime, a place you can bring with you wherever you go. The train takes you back to where you started the journey. It leaves the countryside and the meadow, goes back to the city, to the train platform, back to this room. Now, take a few deep breaths. Stretch your arms and legs. When you're ready, open your eyes and rejoin the circle of friends and parents here at TAG.

During the visualization, most of the kids relax and snuggle up to their parents. Some can't keep their eyes closed. They look around and giggle. One, a 12-year-old, sits up straight as a board with her arms clenched to her chest, her teeth gritted, her eyes focused on a crack in the varnished wood floor.

The leader asks one of the children, "Emily, what toys did you bring with you?" Emily mumbles, "My dog," and the leader says, "Good. And what food did you bring?" She says, "Popcorn." He grins and says, "That sounds yummy! I love popcorn! And who did you bring with you on the picnic?" Emily says, "Grandma." She smiles at the woman she's snuggled up against. "And did you walk up to the dark cabin this time? Did you look in the window?" Emily says, "No. I was too scared." "Oh, I see," he says. "That's a scary place. But you felt safe with your grandma, didn't you?" Emily nods. "Thank you, Emily," the leader says.

"Charles," he says, "what did you have to eat at your picnic?" Charles laughs and says, "Pizza and Coke and jelly-filled donuts!" The leader says, "And who did you bring with you?" "Duke," Charles smirks, "my dog." The leader says, "Did you go up to the dark cabin and look in?" "No," Charles says, "Duke didn't want to go there. He doesn't like forests. He just squatted and pooped in the meadow and we went back onto the train."

The leader says, "I hope he enjoyed the fresh air. Maybe someday you'll want to look in that window. I hope so." Charles shakes his head. Staff note that Charles doesn't take the visualization seriously, but his goofiness still tells them something about what's going on inside. His father just came back into his life after being gone three years; he claims he'd given up drugs and alcohol and wants to be a dad again. Charles's grandparents have heard that kind of talk before, and they worry that Charles will only be hurt again and that their TAG work will be wasted.

After everybody has a chance to talk, they walk down the hall to a room with large plastic tubs full of a variety of small plastic, metal, or wooden toys—cars, alligators, eagles, cows, dogs, horses, cats, people—that would suit a world peopled by characters who are two to six inches tall. Every child gets a sand tray, a plastic tub about two feet square with about two inches of sand in it. The kids can make anything they want. Some brought extra items from home to add to the mix: a set of Pokémon cards, a heart-shaped piece of polished pink granite, a metallic red Hot Wheels Mustang.

For most of TAG 2, the kids create scenes in their sand trays while the parents watch. A child might make a war zone with heavily armed soldiers and men with bazookas battling an army of dinosaurs three times their size. The battle might include tanks and artillery and aircraft shooting down from the sky. A child might make a farm with ducks, cows, and horses, or pretty little houses with gardens, flowers, and birds. Most sand trays include some kind of threat: monsters, supervillains, soldiers, evil-looking cars, snakes, dragons, wolves, bears.

After about twenty minutes, the staff lead small group discussion about the sand trays. A facilitator might say, "Sally, why are those pretty rocks in a pile over there? Why are a large bunny and two smaller bunnies together there? It looks like they're hiding behind the rocks. What are they hiding from?"

Sally might say, "I just think those rocks are pretty. The two little bunnies are me and my brother. They're with their mommy behind the rocks because they're afraid of the dinosaurs." The facilitator might say, "I see what looks like a jewel back in the corner. It's mostly covered with sand. What's the jewel there for?" Sally might say,

"That's buried treasure. The dragon and the dinosaur are guarding it. They don't want us to have it." At the end of the discussion, the leader asks, "If you wanted to name your sand tray, what would you call it?" Sally might say, "Desert rocks" or "Bunnies." The leader then asks Sally's parents what they might call the sand tray. They might say something like, "Standoff" or "The Huddle."

The staff note the trends in each child's sand tray from week to week. Sally's might be all flowers and kittens the next time. By the end of TAG 2, the figures representing her family could be less fearful. Threats could be smaller and farther away. There could be a beach with palm trees, cake, and cookies. Or a child whose trays are always war zones could still be war zones. Either way, the exercise says something about where the child is at, what's going on inside.

Toward the end of TAG 2, parents play in the sand trays with their children. Most parents let the child take the lead and only make suggestions. Sometimes the child wants to play alone, and the parent might claim a corner where they might add something more hopeful than a war zone or a hideout. The last sand tray of the year is a community project. The group is divided in two, and each group of four children and up to eight parents plays in one large sand tray. The children I watched didn't want to collaborate with anyone and claimed their own small territories. The parents added community features and talked to each other about what they wanted: police car, mail truck, doctor, nurse, bank, school. If nothing else, the exercise helps the children see that the place they make for themselves is part of something bigger.

TAG 2 ends with the safe place project. Each child works with parents at home to make something that depicts his or her safe place. On their last day the children present their project to the group. It could be a photo album, a collage, a miniature sand-tray-style diorama in a box, or an abstract sculpture made of playdough or Plasticine, whatever the child and parent decide works for them. The safe place usually includes the child's TAG parents—foster mother, grandparent, uncle, et cetera—and it might have their biological parents in it too. The safe place sometimes includes a pet or a favourite plush toy. It could include the family home and pictures of a vacation trip to Hawaii, Florida, or Nova Scotia.

At the end of the exercise, staff remind the children that they can carry their safe place in their hearts; whenever they feel threatened, they just have to remember it and they can feel safe anywhere. Dr. Bremness says the safe place is something we always have with us, "like a turtle carrying its shell."

After the graduation party, the parents have another meeting on their own with TAG leaders. They talk about their own safe places and where they went on the CASA train. The big question on everyone's minds is: What if my child turns back to the "dark side," follows his addicted mother's example, and all the work we put into TAG is lost? Staff emphasize that TAG isn't magic. Parents can only offer attachment; the child chooses who to attach to. A grandmother whose daughter has already been lost to drugs and crime may have her granddaughter go that way too.

After TAG 2 ends, staff continue one-on-one psychiatric support and play therapy, as needed. TAG 3 is an ongoing monthly facilitated drop-in group for any adult TAG graduates who want to keep their skills sharp or would like continuing support. But TAG doesn't come with a guarantee. Human beings are way more complicated than cars, refrigerators, or computers: you can't send a child back to the factory for a replacement or to get new parts. At the end of TAG, each parent has the expertise to be his or her child's therapist and to continue the TAG process in everyday life. As we'll see in the next chapter, that's a challenging and complicated job, especially for skipped-generation grandparents.

SIX

A Family Dinner: Triggers on the Menu

Parenting, in short, is a dance of the generations.
Whatever affected one generation but has not
been fully resolved will be passed on to the next.
—*Gabor Maté*, When the Body Says No

Nine months ago, child welfare apprehended Johnny (9) and Joey (7) from their drug-addicted parents' home.[1] They live now with their maternal grandparents, Tania and Derek. Johnny holds a fried chicken drumstick in both hands, takes a bite, and looks across the table at his brother. Joey can't sit still. His eyes jump around the room, his head jerks right and left as if he's on high alert for a missile attack. He uses his fork like a bulldozer, pushing his mashed potatoes into a mountain. He rolls peas up the slope one at a time. He

---

1   The scenario described here is a composite based on real examples from people in the TAG program. The names, of course, have been changed.

picks up his water glass and sets it down again without taking a sip.

Suddenly Joey runs away from the table, picks an *Archie* comic off the kitchen counter, and runs back to his chair and sits down. He rolls the magazine into a tube and puts it beside his plate. He shouts, "Tyler wouldn't let me answer! It was my turn and he yelled the answer!" Joey sobs. Tears roll down his cheeks. His chest rises and falls in quick spasms. His voice breaks. "And he laughed at me! The teacher didn't do anything!"

Johnny shouts, "That wouldn't happen if you weren't so slow! And stupid too!" Johnny stands up. "And that's my comic book—give it back!" Johnny reaches across the table and grabs it. Joey yells, "I hate you! I wish you were dead! I don't want a brother anymore!" He runs to his bedroom, sobbing.

Derek's face turns red, his heart beats like a snare drum roll, and he puts a hand on his stomach to dull a stabbing sensation. A voice in his head says, "Here we go again. Every time the family sits down to eat we have more drama!" Derek wants to be the peacekeeper, but he's tried everything already. Recently, he's been so desperate he's yelled right back at Johnny and Joey, "Shut up and sit down!" A few times he's dragged Johnny or Joey upstairs to their rooms. Sometimes he's clenched his arms around his chest and waited for Tania to do something.

Tonight, he remembers where his anger comes from. When he was 6, his father pushed him to read above his grade level. He tried hard to please his father, but it didn't work. He kept a flashlight under his pillow. After he was tucked in for the night, he hid under the comforter and wrestled with big words and long sentences in *The Hobbit* and *Oliver Twist* until his brain ached. People said his father was a genius, a university prof who spent every evening reading and preparing classes. Derek's father told him he was stupid, that he'd have to work as a miner or a ditch-digger his whole life if he didn't try harder. Sometimes Derek's father forced him to read those books out loud to him, and he sent Derek to his room without supper when he choked up and couldn't get a word out.

Johnny's and Joey's fight makes his stomach ache the way it did back then. It's been a struggle, but he's learned to thank his 6-year-old self for trying so hard to please his father, and to honour his father for doing the best he could. So tonight, Derek takes a deep breath, ignores the knot in his throat, and walks around the table to Johnny's place. He gets down on one knee and looks Johnny in the eye. He says, "Johnny, you know Joey is shy. It's hard for him to say things in a large group." Derek pauses for a second and then says, "Could you please go up and tell Joey you're sorry for getting mad? Could you tell him you still love him?"

Johnny stares at Derek. His pupils are small, tight, and black as a coal mine. Bits of chicken fly out of his mouth as he says, "But Joey *is* stupid!" He bangs his fist on the table. "And I'm *not* sorry! You can't make me!" Johnny's hands, arms, mouth, and gut are clenched hard as a fist.

Johnny's full of anger and sadness, but he doesn't know how to name it or control it. Joey stole his comic book, just like when social workers took away his mom, his dad, their apartment, and his big blue bin of Lego. Johnny's body remembers, but he doesn't know how to talk about it. Joey is the only thing he's got left from that apartment where they all lived as a family. He and Joey play well together most of the time. When he plays with Joey, he imagines he's back in that apartment and his parents are sober. But at the dinner table just now, when he looked at Joey across the table, he saw his parents yelling and screaming at each other. He hates Joey for bringing that back.

As Tania watches Joey and Johnny fight, her skull is a vise tightening around her brain. She sees bright flashes one after another, as if a crew of paparazzi were trailing her. She feels a wave of nausea. The forkful of warm mashed potatoes and gravy in her mouth tastes like vomit. She remembers that first migraine headache; it bent her into the fetal position, and she couldn't get up off the cold linoleum for hours. She was 12.

She sees in Johnny her daughter Susan, the kids' mother. At 13, Susan was sexually assaulted in the park on her way home from school. After that, she was a raging tyrant. She'd yell at Tania and Derek if supper wasn't on the table when she walked in the door. She'd throw her plateful of mashed potatoes and gravy, steak, and green beans at the wall if she found gristle in the meat or a speck of skin in the potatoes. She'd light up cigarettes in their non-smoking house and blow the smoke in her parents' eyes. When they reacted, she'd run to the door and slam it on her way out. Three days later she'd stagger home drunk.

Tania and Derek went to family counseling, but they could only get Susan to come with them twice. Tania sees Susan's small, round nose on Johnny's face. Susan is there in the yelling, the name-calling, the running away, the rage.

In between thundering throbs in her head, Tania remembers the summer between grades 7 and 8. She was alone with her older brother on the family farm for hours, sometimes whole days at a time. Several times he forced her into the bushes by the creek and made her perform oral sex on him. Her wrist aches again now, the wrist he twisted to force her down there. The nausea afterwards, the bitter vomit, the stomach acid burning her sinuses. She wanted to tell her parents about it, but she was too full of shame.

Twenty years later, Tania did tell a counsellor and, finally, Derek. The counsellor helped her develop a mantra to calm herself whenever she's triggered. She remembers it now. She breathes slowly, deeply. She tells herself again and again: "I am lovable. It was not my fault. I am a magnificent person." She's used the mantra so often it only takes two or three seconds for her stomach to settle, for the flashes to stop.

When Johnny yells at Derek, "You can't make me!" Tania walks over, gets down on one knee, and kisses his cheek. She puts her arms around him and hugs him tight. He's breathing in short, quick pants. His arms at his sides are stiff as steel. Almost instantly, she feels his muscles start to relax, his breathing become more regular. After about a minute, he rests his head on her shoulder. She feels his warm tears trickle down onto the base of her neck.

Derek sees Tania kiss and hug Johnny, and his bowels are suddenly a hundred pounds heavier. His legs sag under the extra weight. The voice in his head yells, "You blew it again! You're a failure as a father and a grandfather! You couldn't help with Susan, and you're useless with Johnny too!" When he hears Susan's name in his head, he stands up, makes two fists, and cocks his arms as if to slug in the nose the man who wrecked Susan's life, and his and Tania's too. Then he looks around. He hears Joey crying upstairs. "We're all in this together," he tells himself. "I can't just give up and let that rapist win. Joey is alone. Maybe it'll be enough if I just sit with him. I know I can do that."

He goes upstairs. Joey is lying on his bed, curled up in a blanket. He's holding Blackie, the limp little black poodle stuffy he always sleeps with, against his face. Blackie is damp with tears from tail to shoulder. Joey's chest jerks with every sobbing breath. Derek lies down on the bed next to Joey, puts an arm across Joey's back, and lays his head on the pillow beside him. Derek doesn't say anything.

Joey ran up from the dining room table sad and angry. He couldn't have used those words because he doesn't know how to talk about his feelings. When he talked about Tyler, Joey knew in his bones that Johnny has cut him off and put him down all his life. His big brother learned to read before he did, learned to add and subtract before he did, learned to play football and skate before he did. But why does Johnny put him down and make him feel bad about being younger? Joey admires his big brother and wants to be like him, except when Johnny's mean. Joey wishes he'd never been born. He says to himself, inside his head, "My mom and dad never cared about me and now Johnny hates me!"

But with Blackie in his arms, and Grampa Derek curled up around him all warm and snuggly, Joey feels safe again. He can stop crying. He knows he doesn't have to be smart or quick or anything else—he only has to be Joey, and that's enough. He can't quite put this in words, but he knows.

While all this is happening in the dining room and upstairs in Joey's bedroom, all four of them wonder, deep in their unconscious, in their bones and blood and bowels: Where is Susan? Is she safe? Is she living in some drug den with dealers and pimps? Is she selling her body to buy crystal meth? When will they see her again? Will she ever be a normal member of the family? Can she ever be involved in Joey's and Johnny's lives in a positive way, even as an occasional visitor?

Tania and Derek took decades to get where they are, but time alone, even sixty-plus years of it, isn't enough. Many times during their lives they lost their tempers with each other, with Johnny and Joey, with their own children. The TAG program trained them to put grandparent wisdom into action, and it helped them understand their own healing power. In TAG they learned basic brain science and attachment theory. They learned that being calm, aware, in control, and mentally healthy themselves is essential if they are to make good parenting decisions.

Children learn decision-making from parents. Kincare children, whose biological parents modeled bad decision-making, need more than new and better role models. They need help undoing what they learned early in life. Their new parents—in this case, their grandparents—have to do more than merely model for them. TAG parents learn that when a child behaves badly, "he/she is not giving me a hard time; he/she is having a hard time." Children can regress into traumatic memory as quickly as a switch can turn on a light. The grandmother and grandfather have to use their mature prefrontal cortexes to help the children manage their emotions.

Each person has his or her own view of the present, one shaped by the things they've experienced in the past, and this amounts to a sort of life story. At any dinner table of two adults and only one child, six stories are unfolding at the same time. Add a second or third child and you have eight or ten stories, two for each person. In a skipped-generation household in which grandparents are raising two grandchildren, the child in the middle—the kids' absent parent—is there too, past and present, in the minds of his or her parents: "Where is he today?" "Is she drunk or sober?" Add that into the mix and everybody is having twelve stories for dinner, or even more—and that's not even counting the food! That looks like the recipe for a Russian novel. It feels like a war zone sometimes. The grandparents' job is to make peace, without a psychologist (or Tolstoy) on site to help them.

When Tania and Derek were growing up, "Spare the rod and spoil the child" was the slogan of mainstream families. Their parents were born shortly after World War 1, when soldiers were shot for cowardice instead of being treated for "shell shock," which we now know as post-traumatic stress disorder. In the 1970s and '80s, when they raised their own children, the parenting bible was Dr. Benjamin Spock's *The Common Sense Book of Baby and Child Care*. John Bowlby's foundational attachment work was new, and neuroscientists believed brain injuries were permanent. Nobody talked about sex, women were their husband's property, and children were third-class non-citizens. FASD was virtually unknown, fentanyl hadn't been invented, telephones were hard-wired, and mail came in paper envelopes with stamps on them.

Nobody talked about self-care for parents thirty years ago, but for grandparents like Tania and Derek, self-care keeps them sane and increases their chance of surviving until Joey and Johnny are adults. Thirty years ago, Joey and Johnny would have been spanked and banished to their rooms. Spank a child in care today, and you could have the child taken away and get charged with assault.

In TAG, Tania and Derek learned that grandparenting is a long trip into the future. They're on a jet plane with the kids, and when the ride gets bumpy, they all need their seatbelts on. When crisis hits and the oxygen masks drop,

Tania and Derek have to put their masks on first. They have to take care of themselves before they can be of any use to Joey and Johnny. If they don't, their own pre-frontal cortexes will shut down, and all four of them will be in panic mode: fight, flight, or freeze. The dinner table crisis described above could have become a four-way screaming match or a violent free-for-all if Tania and Derek had not learned to take care of themselves ahead of time—if they had not known their own triggers and managed them wisely, if they had simply reacted as their own parents might have done in the 1950s or '60s.

The physical, one-on-one connections that Tania and Derek make with Johnny and Joey solve the dinner table crisis because this is "kit time" applied to real life. It works because it's personal time, one child and one parent present to each other. It can't be a parent and child watching TV together, but it could be parent and child talking about a TV show or a movie and what it says about the child's life.

When Dr. Bremness says kit time changes the child's brain at the molecular level, he's referring to the chemicals each neuron secretes when electric currents travel from cell to cell. Every human brain has about a hundred billion neurons. Each neuron connects with about a thousand others through a thousand synapses. We're born with that many neurons, and how we respond to our environment and the people around us determines what chemicals our brains secrete; our brain, in turn, truncates the synapses we don't use, and sustains the ones we do.

Neuroscientists say the human brain is the most complex thing in the universe, that it contains more synapses than the universe has stars. It contains nerve fibres 1/10,000th the thickness of a sheet of paper, fibres that if laid end to end would be a hundred thousand miles long. When a child is born, these synapses start developing connections, and the connections get stronger and more efficient the more they're used. I've seen images of neurons interacting, pulses of light (representing electrical impulses) traveling down and around a complex network of fibres continuously. These impulses convey information to and from sense organs and other parts of the body, and they regulate every bodily function: images in the eye, smells in the nose, hot and cold on the skin, breathing, digestion, and voluntary and involuntary muscle movement, including the heart. Scientific studies show that early childhood adversity affects brain development so profoundly that it can increase the likelihood of things like cardiovascular disease fifty or sixty years later.[2]

Research also shows that if a child experiences abuse, neglect, or other toxic stresses early in life, the synapses that deal with self-defence and seeking food and attention from grown-ups get overdeveloped and the synapses that enable vocabulary growth and the development of appropriate boundaries for social behaviour, for example,

---

2   This information comes from the presentation that Dr. Judy Cameron (professor of psychiatry, University of Pittsburgh) gave at the Recovery from Addiction Symposium in Banff, Alberta, in October 2012. You can see video of Dr. Cameron's presentation at albertafamilywellness.org.

are stunted or distorted. When a young child experiences abuse or neglect, including sudden and lengthy separation from parents, the impact on the child's brain can be even more profound than the post-traumatic stress disorder an adult suffers after experiencing combat and other forms of life-threatening violence. The child's brain is, in fact, physically injured.

Therapeutic experience also shows that appropriate, positive, personal interaction with such a brain-injured child can repair the damage at the molecular level by encouraging new neural pathways to develop. When Derek and Tania respond appropriately to the conflict between Joey and Johnny, this is what they are doing. In TAG, caregivers learn enough about the science and the practice of helping injured children that they can become live-in therapists for their families while it is still growing and developing.

Whether they get TAG training or not, grandparents who raise grandchildren always have a neurological impact on the young ones in their care. Derek and Tania had to figure out how to move on after traumatic experiences in their own childhoods, but many people their age (or any age, for that matter) simply muddle through, with varying degrees of success. When I was a child, I thought my friends had better family lives than I did. In the early '60s, when John F. Kennedy was president, the media contributed to the myth of the Kennedys living in a Camelot-like fantasy world in which even the rain fell only at convenient times. But King Arthur's own family was dysfunctional to the core. The truth is closer to a cartoon drawing I saw on a bulletin board in a psychologist's office: one man sits in a big auditorium full of empty chairs, and a banner across the stage says, "Annual Conference of Non-dysfunctional Families." Was that man there to figure out how other families did it, or was he simply deluded, thinking his own family was perfect?

For many families, "dysfunctional" isn't a strong enough word. What do we call sexual abuse, physical violence, alcoholism, drug addiction, abandonment, and the like that perpetuates itself generation after generation? For example, Canada's Truth and Reconciliation Commission, or TRC, concluded that the residential school system was a form of "cultural genocide," and the racism that drove it continues today. Indigenous people are not the only ones in Canada to suffer from generational trauma and dysfunction, but they are massively overrepresented in the country's prisons, foster homes, and grandparent-headed, skipped-generation families. Yet Indigenous peoples in Canada and around the world have for thousands of years embodied cultural practices rooted in children's attachment to their extended families, and until colonization their networks of family support and connection were vibrant and strong.

SEVEN

Indigenous Grandparenting: One Foot in Each Canoe

Who's to determine whether they are at risk? Our children, we raise 'em to be independent. I shot a gun when I was eight years old, supervised by my dad. And when we're twelve, thirteen, we're old enough to go out on our own.... You gotta survive, gotta make a living, gotta know how to hunt, how to garden, stuff like that.

—*A Cree grandmother*

"We were counting the number of children that call us grandparents," Chris told me. The total was thirty-five. He said over a hundred kids have lived in his home for varying lengths of time and that it's common for twenty-five people or more to stay overnight in his family's three-bedroom home in south-western Ontario. "There's no guarantee even *I'll* get a bed!" he laughed. "Everybody crashes where they can."

In Indigenous cultures, "grandfather" and "grand-mother" are fluid terms. I've been in sweat lodges where the Elder says to the fire-keeper, "Bring in the grandfathers." A shovel appears in the entrance of the lodge with two or three large, round stones on it. When the flap closes over the entrance, their red glow is the only light in the lodge. In their tradition, these stones represent the spirits of past generations and ancestral wisdom handed down for millennia. They also represent the physical and spiritual unity of the Earth, all humanity, and the Creator.

In Chris's world, it's enough that the children he takes in are Indigenous. In this context, "grandfather" and "grandmother" are not mere biological references but shorthand, as if to say, "These people are my connection to my heritage, which is the source of my identity."

He gave me an example of how complicated the terminology in his family could get if someone wanted to be technical about it. "My wife grew up in what I call an extended family. So the fellow who lost his twins to Children's Aid called my wife 'aunt,' although he's her cousin. Because she's an aunt, I'm basically called the uncle. Children's Aid asked if they had any family that wanted to step forward. So we put our names in, and they said, 'Yeah, you qualify, and we're gonna put you through the kinship program.' The twins we've adopted are now my daughters. Because of the way my wife grew up, we were thought of as aunt and uncle to the father. But really, we're our adopted daughters' third cousins."

They could just as easily have been called "great-aunt" and "great-uncle." But "grandparents" fits too. It's simpler, acknowledges the age differences, and suits the culture.

An Indigenous grandmother I met in Alberta, a survivor of ten years in a residential school—I'll call her Dorothy—told me her grandmother raised about forty children. "This is really normal in our families," she says. "In our Indigenous culture, we have a belief that children are on loan to you from the Creator and it's this community's responsibility to make sure children grow up. This is why grandparents, aunts, uncles—everybody—get involved with bringing up children."

Dorothy said she met many Indigenous people who were taken into non-Indigenous foster homes and had "wonderful upbringings." But, she said, "There was always a search, always a longing: Who am I? Where do I come from?" Her aunt gave a baby up for adoption in the 1940s. He was raised by a Scottish family who never allowed him to talk about his Aboriginal heritage. He learned Gaelic and all their family values and customs, but he knew something was missing. Dorothy said people like him may spend a lifetime searching for their Indigenous roots, and some never find them.

That Scottish family could have loved their adopted son as much as they loved their own biological children, Dorothy said, but would that have been any different from a Catholic nun who taught in a residential school, if she actually loved him? Dorothy mentioned the Indigenous boy former Prime Minister Jean Chrétien and his wife adopted and raised. "They gave him every-thing they could," she said. "But they could not give him his identity, his roots." I heard several stories like this at the final public session of the TRC in Edmonton in 2014. Thousands of survivors of residential schools, their children and grandchildren, and many others wept at the stories of multi-generational trauma caused by the residential school system: children taken from parents and forced to live in squalor, suffer abuse, and sometimes die of neglect, disease, and despair, and for generations afterwards, whole communities rife with drugs and alcohol addictions, poverty, violence, and self-loathing.

Racism was the foundation on which the residential school system was built, the reason that these Indigenous children were cut off from their spiritual, linguistic, cultural roots. In Canada, we trace the system back to Sir John A. Macdonald, who said Canada should "kill the Indian, but save the man." Others after him talked about this as "killing the Indian in the child." This is a common feature of colonization, and there's an English word for it: "deracination," which simply means cutting people off from their ethnic and cultural foundations. In the Americas as a whole, what I call "The Racism Charter" came out of the Vatican in the form of a series of papal bulls proclaiming the "Doctrine of Discovery" in the fif-teenth century. Typical among them was one by Pope Nicholas V in 1455 justifying European nations' efforts "to invade, search out, capture, vanquish, and subdue all…

enemies of Christ," and to take their land and "reduce their persons to perpetual slavery."[1]

I told Dorothy how my dad died in 2006. He was 92 years old. On the death certificate, it said he was one-quarter "American Indian." My family has been unable to find any other documentation to support that claim. When I was growing up in the United States, my parents told me my paternal grandmother was Cherokee, but I didn't know what that meant. When I asked my mother ten years ago, she said that if my dad wanted to, he could have claimed treaty rights; all four of us kids could've had free health care and post-secondary education because we were Indigenous.[2] I asked her why he didn't, and she told me that in those days, Indians in Oklahoma were even lower on the social scale than black people. Indigenous people, like the descendants of slaves, were taught to be ashamed of their identity.

Dorothy nodded. "And that's the way it still is in Canada! You have the Caucasian, then the immigrants, and then the Indigenous people. We're still at the bottom of the totem pole!"

---

1   For a concise summary see Steve Newcomb, "Five Hundred Years of Injustice: The Legacy of 15th Century Religious Prejudice," *Shaman's Drum* (fall 1992), 18–20, or https://www.gilderlehrman.org/content/doctrine-discovery-day-1493. Spanish conquistadores put this hateful theology into practice by gathering groups of Incan, Aztec, and Mayan people, reading a proclamation in Spanish and Latin ordering them to worship Jesus, and then slaughtering or enslaving everyone who didn't kneel before the crucifix. In the 1990s and early 2000s, Catholics and others petitioned Pope John Paul II to rescind these papal bulls and recognize the rights of Indigenous peoples, but those bulls have still not been rescinded.

2   Health care and post-secondary education would have been free, but it would have been second-rate at best. See the US National History of Medicine website, www.nlm.nih.gov/exhibition/if_you_knew/index.html.

The TRC's final report included ninety-four recommendations to address racism in Canada and promote healing in the aftermath of the residential schools. The first one would ensure that Indigenous children apprehended by child welfare departments know their heritage and stay connected to their culture, whether they go into foster homes, group homes, Kinship Care, or are adopted out. Most provinces already have policies like this in effect. Foster mother Linda Krauskopf (whose story we heard in chapter 5) told me about the intergenerational impact policies like this can have. She was caring for an Indigenous foster child whose father had come to visit. When the child's father, accompanied by a band Elder, came to visit, Linda asked the Elder if he would teach the girl something about their band's culture. "He looked at me and said, 'To tell you the truth, we don't have anything cultural in our band.'" But because the girl had already been able to re-establish her cultural connections, she was able to dance for him and teach him what she knew.

The history of child welfare agencies, though, is rife with racism. Chris told me that when he and his wife were in their early fifties, they applied to be foster parents. "We said we'd like to make sure Native children go into Native homes, and we wanted to be that Native or Aboriginal home. They sent us a letter where they said we were too old to do that." Yet here Chris and I were, talking to each other at the CANGRANDS annual camp, where I'd just met a great-grandmother and over thirty other grandparents, many of whom were well over 60! So I asked about that.

Since the 1950s, Chris said, "Aboriginal people and Children's Aid have had a feud going on." The claim he was too old was really a reflection of "the whole racial issue, but they would never admit that. I don't blame them for not admitting that, but that's reality. Chris said that Children's Aid later "recanted," or at least modified their position, and told him that he and his wife were young enough to adopt after all. At the time, he said, "adoption was not on the radar screen," but "it didn't matter to us. We were gonna protect these two little girls." He told me they also adopted a boy the same age as the twins, so at that time they were raising three 7-year-olds, in addition to the girl they adopted at the age of 2, who was then 26.

"We have four of our own children," he said, "and four officially adopted children. Other street kids who stay with us briefly and call us mom and dad, we respect that." Those children, he said, have lived with them any-where from a couple of months to ten years. "Usually, it was teenagers being teenagers and parents being parents and the conflict got out of hand. Usually, the kids were kicked out of the home and, not having any place to go, they stopped by our place. We said, 'We'll put you up until you get on your feet.'" Sometimes the kids' parents came to stay for a while too.

I assumed that all these people knew to come to Chris's house because he and his wife lived in a small, tight-knit community, maybe on a reserve, where everybody knows everybody else. Chris laughed, "If you call a city with over 350,000 people a tight community, we do!" He said they used to live in North Bay, and they spend time on a reserve too. But plenty of Aboriginal people live in his city, he said, and word just gets around.

"Many non-Aboriginal families would do a good job" of raising these Aboriginal children, Chris said—"maybe even a more effective job than we would. But what we try to instill in our children is to understand our way of life and where we came from and how to be accepted in both societies. That's the major difference: teaching who we are."

One piece of that is language. Chris said he and his wife don't speak Iroquois fluently, "but we want to pass on to [the children] the little we have so that if they want to pursue the language later in life, they can." Ceremonies are another piece. One simple principle in all the ceremonies, he said, is that respect is given only to the Creator. "You don't say thank you. You don't say please pass the salt. All those things are given because the only one who gets praised at that table is the Creator."

They do smudges for prayer, cleansing, and meditation. There's a special ceremony when someone dies, Chris explained, "to make sure the spirit has left the Earth and has gone on to the spirit world, because if that spirit doesn't leave, it can create mischief for you, mischief for others. And sometimes the spirit is just caught in a world and doesn't want to be there. They know what the spirit world is like. It's sort of like a garden of Eden compared to where they are. So they want to get there, and we help them get there."

As well, Chris and his wife teach kids what's expected at ceremonies and what not to do. At funerals, he said, most people get a black ribbon and put a pin through it. "That tells the rest of the world you're in mourning and you're a relative of the deceased." He said Christianity told them to take the pin and ribbon off and throw them on the casket to indicate the grieving is over. "But in the Aboriginal community, we know grieving does not end when a person is placed in the ground. You still miss them. And we say nothing made of silver is supposed to go in the coffin with them. So by throwing that pin in there, you're actually playing with the occult. We don't want any witchcraft coming out of that."

Chris said that, for them, mourning involves a ten-day feast, followed by another feast a year later; this says that mourning is over and the spirit of the dead person has moved on. "And if people do not stop mourning then, we have a ten-year feast. That's not put on for everybody, just for people who are still grieving. If your child or spouse passed away, you'd probably have feelings for them ten years later."

Chris told me something else I didn't know, even though I've taken a granddaughter to powwows and powwow dances: different tribes have different powwow practices. "The Iroquois, the Hopi, the Cree, the Ojibway go to powwows," he said. "But whoever is putting it on is putting something on for everybody. We say to our children, 'Be very careful. This is what you've gotta watch out for, because this is a celebration for all Aboriginal people, and not all are the same.' " Which makes sense, of course, because Christian religions are different from each other too, and so are celebrations of any kind, say in Japan, different from celebrations in Ethiopia.

One very visible feature of Aboriginal culture, once you know how to look for it, Chris said, is how Aboriginal artists and craftspeople "sign" their work by leaving the small imperfections that often come about in a handmade piece of art. "If you can make something for a dollar and sell it for a hundred dollars, you'd be surprised how many people will make it, [but] there's a lot of stuff on the market that isn't Aboriginal made." He said, "If it's done by a true Aboriginal artist, there's always a flaw somewhere in that article. There's a bead turned over backwards. There's a bead that's a different colour....If you were to get an heirloom and someone says it's two hundred years old and it's made by so and so, all you have to do is look for that flaw. If there are no flaws, 'Oh, that's nice,' and that is all you say about it."

The rawhide fringes on beaded Aboriginal jackets? They're not just decoration, Chris explained. "If you were out on a journey all by yourself and you got cut, that thing would provide a tourniquet to stop the bleeding. And if you needed a Band-Aid very quickly, just pull on it, and it's a ready-made Band-Aid."

Chris also told me a few things about alcohol and drunkenness that they teach their grandkids. "A lot of people make fun of the term 'firewater,' " he said. That goes back to when Aboriginal people figured out how to check the quality of the alcohol they would bargain for at trading posts. If it burst into flame when they lit a match over it, they knew it was good; if not, they knew it had been watered down. He said they teach the children how to think about a person they might see lying down drunk in a park. "That must be an awful way of life," he tells them, but "the Creator put that person in this world for a purpose: to teach others they shouldn't follow his path. You take a look and see how beat up he is and what kind of life he's living and you say to yourself, 'I don't want to live that kind of life.' He is not to be thought of as evil, because there's probably not an evil bone in his body."[3]

Chris continued: "We tell them there is good and evil in this world. If there wasn't evil, you wouldn't know good. Here's what the missionaries did to us, we say, but that doesn't mean all missionaries are bad. This is what some of the white men have done. Some of them are bad; some are very good. Some are gonna treat you like a brother, but you gotta be careful. Make sure you understand their intentions. Sometimes they're friends with you because they want something. Sometimes they're friends because they genuinely want to be your friend. We say there's actually two roads, and you gotta have one foot in both canoes at the same time. You've got to understand how the white man exists and you gotta live in that world because that's probably most of your world."

---

3   The devastation that alcohol has wrought in Indigenous communities is profound and intergenerational. Chris told me that several of the grandchildren he's raised are either suffering from or are suspected of having FASD.

Dorothy straddled both worlds when she was a social worker within the child welfare system, but the strain took its toll, and she couldn't do it for long. "They thought I was from Mars!" she said. "Such a different mindset. Not even trying to understand our culture and where we come from. Always that superiority, the 'we-know-better' about your children. I'll argue until I'm blue in the face, even until I die: Leave these kids with their families! Yes, they may need help. Take the kids and put them with family!"

Dorothy told me about a family with three kids, the youngest 4 years old. The oldest one was physically abused for years and watched his stepfather abuse his younger sisters too. The boy's loyalty to his mother and the step-dad kept him from saying anything, but he finally spoke up. He told his teacher; a social worker confirmed the story with one of the sisters; and then child welfare "just swooped in and took the kids," Dorothy said. "I could not believe it! Why would you do this to children?" Instead of taking the kids to their grandmother, who eventually did take them in, the kids were split into different foster homes. "That little four-year-old was so traumatized she was catatonic the next day." Dorothy said, "It's a good thing it was an Aboriginal worker who apprehended them," or it would've been even worse.

They do this to Aboriginal kids all the time, she said. "Once they're in the system, you lose them forever. They will be so damaged! I have never seen a good foster home yet, where kids have been treated well. They always have other kids. Their natural kids are always treated a little bit more special than [the Aboriginal] kids. They are never treated equally. That's the story I've gotten from every adult who's come through the foster homes, the 'serial' homes. Why don't they just leave them in the dysfunctional Aboriginal home? That's just as dysfunctional and harmful. Leave them in the dysfunctional family home and work with them. It's less costly for the children and their future, less costly on the parents, less costly on the government."[4]

Dorothy said the system took six months to get counseling for the mother and four months for the children. The mother's counseling was a forty-five-minute drive away, and the children had to miss school. Until the grandmother fought for something better. The grandmother refused to take the older boy out of school for the appointments because of the stigma attached to seeing a counsellor. The grandmother provided a good, safe home for the family, but Dorothy said it was six months before anyone even gave the grandmother a questionnaire to begin the process of determining whether her home was safe.

In that questionnaire, Dorothy saw yet more evidence of racism. "It says 'Registered Indian,' but we are not Indians. We are Indigenous; Indians are from India!" She said, "I'm very passionate about equality, about them treating us the way we should've been treated from day one. We have been nothing but gracious hosts, and what

---

4 A different perspective—that of another social worker whose caseload mostly involves supporting families so they can change and keep their own children—is given in chapter 15.

do they do? They've stolen our land. The treaties were not about land deals, they were about the peaceful sharing of whatever's here. And they've just taken and taken and taken! If you wanna know about inclusion and diversity, look to Indigenous people. Look how we welcomed you to this land."

After she retired from social work, Dorothy began facilitating weekend workshops for other residential school survivors, "to educate our people that we are not a flawed people. There's nothing wrong with us....No. It's our history. We've been wounded. We've had 150 or 200 years of disruption in our culture, but we're coming back. Many people don't understand what life was like prior to contact: really beautiful country. Ten thousand years we've been here!"

Dorothy talked about life on Turtle Island[5] 500 years ago, how the West was "a metropolis of trade and commerce" and Aboriginal people were entrepreneurs before the word was even thought of. "The trading that went on, north, south, east—the trails are still here. They're discovering towns and cities all over the place. All the major cities across Canada—Edmonton has an 8,000-year history of Indigenous people gathering. Same as Winnipeg. They recently discovered more artifacts in an area they didn't expect, where there was settlement 5,000 to 6,000 years ago." And seven years ago, she said, they discovered a whole townsite in Toronto.

---

5   The name by which some Indigenous peoples have historically referred to North America.

"I know my people gathered here in the summers for ceremonies for this and that, for trade. There were Pueblo tribes who came up north. The Navajo?" she said, "One Navajo Elder from New Mexico said, 'We're not Navajo. We are Dene. We've been separated from our relatives for 200 years. Because of that border, we're not allowed to leave the reserves.' "

I told her of a trip I took through the Four Corners area of the American Southwest. I stopped at a roadside trading post and told a man selling blankets that I was from Alberta. He talked about Hobbema (now renamed Maskwacis) and other places near Edmonton as if he just lived down the street from me and the people in Hobbema were his family.

"That's how we were and still are," Dorothy said. "The powwows and those ceremonial things they did—they shared stories, and the trade was very strong in North America. And peacemaking. Where do you think the treaty process came in? Indigenous people were already into treaty-making between tribes so they wouldn't war against each other. They married into each other's tribes to make sure peace was kept. Peaceful existence was the ultimate."

She paused, looked me in the eye, and said, "It was always about relationships. Would I, as a grandmother, war against a different tribe where my grandchildren were? No way! Because of our value on our grandchildren we would go to the ninth end to make peace."

She told me it doesn't matter whether on a reserve or in a city: grandparents always play a central role in the community. "No matter where you go," she says, "grand-parents have a huge role in the upbringing of our children. That's how we pass on the wisdom and knowledge, through the grandmothers and grandfathers."

EIGHT

On the Reserve

Home is the place where, when you have to go there,
They have to take you in.

—*Robert Frost*

The trembling aspen forest both sides of Highway 44 north of Westlock, Alberta, glows yellow green on this May morning, more like the colour of golden sunshine than the dark green they'll be in a week or two. The air is clear and fresh with the exhalation of newborn leaves. The fire season will start before the month is over, but today the cloudless sky is as blue as the Pacific Ocean. It's the Victoria Day weekend, and I'm driving to visit an Indigenous friend. I've lived in Alberta over forty years, but this is only the second time I've driven this far north, into what most non-Indigenous people would call the middle of nowhere. I've had no reason to go this way before. After all, I'm a city guy, except for when I take a vacation trip to the Rockies or to a friend's farm in central Alberta.

It's a three-hour drive from where I live in Edmonton. After the first hour, there's not much to see except trees, the occasional gravel road, and one truck stop. But for the car I'm in and the newly paved highway, this looks, feels, and smells like wilderness.

When I step inside, my friend's house looks like the type of suburban home you'd find in any Canadian city. Then I see a frozen fish on the kitchen counter. I look closer. The frosty, dark grey surface isn't made up of fish scales. And the thing has no fins, nor any knife marks where fins used to be. It's an oval shape with a flat spot on one edge. That flat spot on the narrow part of the oval is pink, like a steak. "Oh, that's a beaver tail," my friend says. "We got that out maybe for supper."

I'm afraid my American-ness is showing. I was born and raised south of the forty-ninth parallel. Down there, the national animal—the bald eagle—is a protected species. Subconsciously, I assumed Canada's national animal must be protected too, not because they're rare but because they symbolize Canada itself. My friend tells me that if people didn't hunt and trap them, beavers would overrun the place. For Indigenous people, he says, the beaver tail is a good source of meat, and, two hundred and fifty years after the peak of the fur trade, beaver fur is still great for making coats, hats, and mitts. I notice some small pieces of black fur on the living room table; he says that's bearskin.

In his backyard, he shows me a 12-foot diameter teepee he uses to dry skins and an oil-drum-sized plastic barrel for softening skins. In his garage he shows me muskrat, beaver, skunk, and moose hides in various stages of stretching. The moose hide, he said, when finished, could sell for up to $1,500. In the west-facing window I see several pairs of small testicles hanging from nails. He says those are really scent glands, and they're great to attract game on hunting trips. Their secretions are also used to make powerful traditional medicine. He shows me his freezer, packed full of moose sausage, beaver tails, and other wild meat he's hunted in the nearby forest.

He tells me of a time he took his 3-year-old son hunting and they almost shot a beaver in a game preserve. He wasn't sure where the boundary was, and then he saw the sign. He told his son that because of the sign, they weren't allowed to shoot the beaver; it was protected. His son didn't understand how a sign could do that, and so the boy said, "Why don't we just move the sign then?" My friend told his son that part of learning to hunt as an Indigenous person is following the rules. Not just the Indigenous rules about honouring the animal, using all parts of the animal's carcass, and thanking the Creator, but the non-Indigenous rules about game preserves.

One of the rules my friend lives by is sharing with relatives and friends. Wherever I went with him, he brought a bag of frozen wild meat from his freezer and gave it away. Witnessing this gave me a glimpse of what it means to be Indigenous in rural Alberta. I brought with me on the trip some copies of my book, *Human on the Inside*, to give each person I interviewed. My friend told me two of those people were more traditional and that I should give them tobacco too, even though one of them doesn't smoke.

After supper at his house, he and I drive for an hour. About fifty minutes is on smooth, well-maintained asphalt, a primary highway. Then we turn onto a gravel road, drive past the band office and into a flat aspen forest with a few jack pines scattered through it. Houses are far apart, maybe a kilometre or more. The dusty road we're on and the others we intersect have no names or signs, and I don't see any numbers on the houses. My friend navigates by instinct and memory. He knows this place as well as he knows his own skin.

We pull into an empty driveway beside a white split-level house. A pit bull is tethered to a post in the middle of the front yard. My friend asks me to stay in the car while he looks around; he says it feels odd that ours is the only car in the driveway, since that must mean nobody's home, even though he'd arranged for us to meet someone there. When he gets to the front door, a woman looks out the upstairs window. He says something to her. He goes in the house and comes out a few minutes later. He says the person to interview isn't home, that we'll have to try tomorrow.

He says he smelled weed in the house and suspected the grandmother probably didn't feel comfortable even being in the house with marijuana smoke. He says the woman I saw in the window was her daughter; she couldn't raise her own children because of a drug addiction.

He has another idea. We drive a few more minutes and pull into a wide driveway covered with freshly laid gravel at least two inches deep. It's clear from the many outbuildings and the various tools carefully placed next to them that this is a working farm and that whoever runs it takes pride in its tidy appearance.

We go into the house. My friend's uncle sits at the dining room table with a 15-year-old boy. Above them a large flat-screen television is mounted on the wall. My friend introduces me as an author who's writing a book about grandparenting, and the uncle tells me about his own book about Indigenous medicine. He shows me a copy. It's a beautiful softcover book published in the United States.

The uncle tells me that his mother took in Indigenous foster children as well as grandchildren. She raised 13 or 14 grandchildren, in addition to 12 children of her own. He laughs when he remembers what a madhouse it was with so many kids in the house. The first ones started coming when he was 15. He says he still resents that she raised all those children. What made it worse for him is that she left most of her possessions to the grandchildren while he and his siblings got nothing. He imagines his mom thinking, "Oh, they're young. Might as well give it to them. You guys are doing okay now." He laughs. "That was the only downfall of raising grandchildren!"

I ask him why his mother took in so many kids. She had no choice, he says, because that was the only way to prevent them from being given to non-Indigenous families, who would raise them in a totally different faith and culture. He says, "Every religion is actually a connection to the Great Spirit or God. It doesn't matter which religion you put on; it's the same connection, the same energy. Doesn't matter if you're a Jehovah, a Roman Catholic, or whatever you want to be. But really, Natives should be learning their own traditional stuff." If they did, he said, "You wouldn't see so many things going wrong with all those people."

"Ninety-five per cent of these get in trouble after they're eighteen," he says. "A young guy between eighteen and twenty-five might commit a big crime. Where's the parents? They're not gonna do anything now. They're already pissed off at welfare for takin' the kids away. And welfare's gonna stand back. They won't do nothing. They should be paying for the lawyers. They're the ones who took the kids away. They should be fully responsible for something that goes wrong. Let's say somebody's charged for murder. Do you think welfare'll say, 'Well, we raised that kid, took her away from her parents'? They don't care. They just scrap 'em and go grab some other kids."

He claims Indigenous kids have been taken by child welfare simply because the parents tried to discipline them. He talks about a boy who complained to his teacher that his dad was going to spank him: the teacher starts asking questions, and "all of a sudden," he says, "welfare'll just grab 'em and go to court. If you want 'em back, get a lawyer." But the parents can't afford a lawyer, and the children don't know why their parents aren't fighting for them.

"There's one here last summer," he says. "They took the kid, and the parents never got 'im back until Christmastime! She sold a few groceries and that. The neighbours said, 'Oh, she's starvin' the kids!' Her six kids weren't starving. She was trying to make ends meet." When welfare workers checked the freezer and the fridge in the home, they were full, he says, but a second neighbour claimed the mother was selling food. "No questions asked," he said. "They just—whoosh, like pit bulls going in to get 'em. That's what I call them." He laughs, but not because it's funny. That's how he releases, bit by bit, the anger he carries in his bones.

He told me his own stepchild complained to her teacher that he was mean. He said she wouldn't do her homework and chores around the house. "Welfare picked her up. They didn't drop her off at the bus stop. They didn't tell us anything." The family took welfare to court, and after four months and $5,000 for a lawyer, the judge ruled in their favour, and they got the child back.

"The welfare system's garbage, in my books," he says. He mentions a great-grandmother who raised two little kids but had to give them up because she lived on a pension and couldn't afford them anymore. The kids went back to their mother, even though the mother's home was unsafe. "If a relative wants to keep the kids, welfare should say, 'Okay, you keep them and we'll pay you the same we pay the rest.' But they won't. Because if you keep them, you're on your own."

I ask him if he thinks the welfare system is simply a continuation of the residential schools. "We *know* that," he replies without hesitation, just as certainly as he knows the sky is blue and the lake is wet. One of the few differences, he says, is that the churches were involved before. When he was 6 years old, he says, "the father and the nuns" came from the mission to take him and other kids away; "and if a parent does not let them go, then the police come right behind them." He said the mission routinely did tonsillectomies on the kids, and when they did his, he got an infection and had to spend the whole summer in the hospital while the others went home. The operation took away his voice for a while and damaged it permanently, he said. His voice sounded normal to me, but a deeper damage was evident in every comment he made.

He says his mom and dad came to the mission on horseback one Christmas Day to visit him and his siblings, bringing gifts and food. "They weren't allowed. They were arguing right outside. We could see them from the window. They had turned their horses around. They were gonna get escorted by the police if they didn't leave."

"The worst part of it," he says, is that if a kid didn't like some kind of food, "they shoveled it down your throat. Two, three bigger boys hold you down and the nun forks it all the way down your throat. Even if you throw up, they'll still keep throwin' it in." He told me that even now, fifty years later, he still can't eat corn or tomatoes.

Before I leave his house, I decide to give him a copy of *Human on the Inside*, my book about prisons and the criminal justice system. The orange and black cover photo shows a hand reaching through the bars of a prison cell. "After residential school, *that* would be easy," he says, pointing at the photo. "At least in there they don't force-feed you corn and tomatoes!"

All eleven of his siblings went to residential school. The last of these institutions finally closed in 1996, but for Indigenous people, the deadly racism on which that system was built continues today. During the so-called '60s Scoop, the federal government authorized the provinces to intervene on reserves when they thought Indigenous children were at risk. By some accounts, up to 90 per cent of the children on reserves simply disappeared into the child welfare system. Grandparents stepped in then—and they continue to step in now—to keep their grandchildren out of the system. But there were way more Indigenous children apprehended than Indigenous grandparents to place them with, and so many were placed in foster homes and adopted into non-Indigenous families.

In *Disrobing the Aboriginal Industry*, Frances Widdowson and Albert Howard say any claim that social workers were participating in "cultural genocide" during the '60s Scoop is based on an incomplete reading of the facts. They write: "In the 1950s the government became aware of the dysfunctional character of aboriginal communities, with high rates of child neglect, pedophilia, and incest. With the level of drunkenness that existed in these communities at this time, many families were unable to provide a safe and loving home for children and it was the government's responsibility to intervene."[1] They concede, however, that the policy suffered from "poor implementation."[2]

But if the '60s Scoop wasn't itself a racist policy, the socio-political culture of the day was thoroughly racist, and elements of that racism continue today. Federally, Indigenous people got the right to vote in 1960; the last province to follow suit was Quebec, in 1969. Indigenous women are prime targets for sexual assault and murder even now. Violence against Indigenous women was a key issue during the 2015 federal election, the results of which led to the creation of the National Inquiry into Missing Indigenous Women and Girls. The rates of addiction, poverty, incarceration, suicide, infant mortality, and unemployment are much higher among Indigenous people, and life expectancy is much lower.[3] Two hundred and fifty years of racism has had a profound, multi-generational impact. Is it any wonder, then, that child welfare departments apprehend a disproportionate number[4] of Indigenous children?

---

1   Frances Widdowson and Albert Howard, *Disrobing the Aboriginal Industry: The Deception behind Indigenous Cultural Preservation* (Montreal: McGill-Queen's University Press, 2008), 165.

2   Ibid.,166.

3   As of February 2013, Indigenous prisoners made up 23.2 per cent of the total population in Canada's federal prisons; 4 per cent of the Canadian population is Indigenous. See Office of the Correctional Investigator, "Annual Report, 2016–2017," http://www.oci-bec.gc.ca/cnt/rpt/pdf/annrpt/annrpt20162017-eng.pdf. See also, "Social Conditions of Indigenous People," Canadian Encyclopedia, http://www.thecanadianencyclopedia.ca/en/article/native-people-social-conditions/.

4   Statistics Canada reported in 2016 that 7 per cent of all children in Canada under the age of fourteen were Indigenous, yet they accounted for 48 per cent of all foster children in that age group. See Annie Turner, "Insights on Canadian Society: Living arrangements of Aboriginal children aged 14 and under," https://www.statcan.gc.ca/pub/75-006-x/2016001/article/14547-eng.htm.

As long as racism is a fact in Canada, it's really a moot point whether or not government actions like the '60s Scoop are racist. Racism is the underlying reality. At the final public sessions of the Truth and Reconciliation Commission in Edmonton in 2014, I heard Justice Murray Sinclair say that anti-Indigenous racism will end only when ordinary people can no longer comfortably make racist comments in the privacy of their homes, in front of their children. The day before those proceedings opened, Edmonton City Council unanimously voted to proclaim a "year of reconciliation," emphatically acknowledging that anti-Indigenous racism has been a fact of life in Edmonton for a long time and still is.

In January 2016, the Canadian Human Rights Tribunal ruled that the level of federal funding for child welfare on reserves is 38 per cent less than other child welfare in Canada. In a June 2, 2017, article in the *Ottawa Citizen*, Dr. Cindy Blackstock, a prominent academic and Indigenous activist, noted that "there are at least three times the number of First Nations children in state care today than at the height of residential schools." Since the ruling, the tribunal has issued more rulings calling the Trudeau government to account for its failure to comply with the original order to end racial discrimination against First Nations children. The government has decided to appeal instead of taking action to address the issue. On September 23, 2017, *The Globe and Mail* published an open letter to Prime Minister Trudeau calling on the government to comply with the ruling. It was signed by Murray Sinclair, Sheila Fraser, Bob Rae, and thirty-eight others.[5]

More Indigenous children are still apprehended than there are Indigenous families to take them in. On that reserve in northern Alberta, I heard three themes over and over: that the child welfare system is dysfunctional; that it's normal for grandparents to take their grandchildren into their homes to raise; and that cultural practices and spiritual teachings are essential to these children's well-being.

One grandmother I talked to, Ruth, was an addictions counsellor and a registered social worker. She had worked in the child welfare system both on and off reserve. She'd raised two grandchildren, one for sixteen years and one for eight; now the girl is 19 and the boy 15. Ruth's husband died in 1999, and she's been single since then. Hers was the split-level house with the pit bull tethered out front. My friend took me back there the next day.

A teenage boy leaves the house as we come in. A woman in her early sixties welcomes us to her dining room and offers us bowls of steaming-hot moose stew: golf-ball sized chunks of white potato, carrot, and moose in gravy thick enough to eat with a fork. Bannock hot from the oven is piled high on a plate in front of us. But I'm still full from breakfast—and besides, I know if I eat anything with wheat flour in it, I'd bloat up with enough gas to get us back to town. So I decline the food and take a cup of

---

5   The federal budget unveiled in February 2018 finally included funding to begin to address this issue.

tea. My friend, though, must have an extra stomach. He scoops stew into his mouth, one spoonful after another, as if he hadn't eaten all week. He compliments the cook on how tender the meat is. He says he hardly has to chew it. He's a wild-meat expert, and he wants to know her secret. He nods, puts another scoop in his mouth, and picks up a chunk of bannock in his free hand so it's ready to go in as soon as he has room.

All the while, a woman about 40 years old stands in the corner of the kitchen, near the oven. She doesn't say anything to us and seems not to be doing anything but standing there. Nobody introduces her to me, but I soon discover she's the mother of the grandkids. I offer Ruth a copy of *Human on the Inside* and thank her for talking to me. I ask her if it was a hard choice to take the kids in. She purses her lips and says, "Well, it had to be done, because I didn't want them going to child welfare." The 40-year-old woman mumbles something I can't make out. I ask Ruth if she has an official guardianship order, and Ruth says yes, she went to court and got the papers. The woman in the corner says, "I went somewhere else. I wasn't allowed to take my daughter with me."

Ruth grits her teeth. She says we should end the interview. I say okay and look at my friend as he nonchalantly chews his bannock. I wait. Suddenly, the mother walks to the front door, says "See ya!" and leaves.

"See how she hangs out?" Ruth says. "She has no place to go. She's still an addict. She's been an addict since she was sixteen." Ruth says her daughter would leave for months at a time and never tried to get help for her addiction. The children's father was an addict too. Both of them were on illicit prescription drugs. "When the boy was seven," she says, "I was working at the women's shelter." Her daughter came there with the boy, and he said to Ruth, "Can I come to live with you? I don't want to live with my mom and dad anymore because they're always high." At that time Ruth had already had the boy's sister for eight years.

Ruth tells me from the beginning she encouraged both of them to find strength in their Indigenous heritage, as she does. She smudged with them every day, and took them to ceremonies as much as she could. Ruth herself often goes to sweats, and the grandson's a drummer. These cultural practices were the medicine they needed to heal and move on, she says. Her granddaughter "got messed up for a couple of years with addictions," but she's been clean a year and a half, living in Edmonton on her own and attending a career training college. Ruth tells me that she can speak Cree, but she didn't pass it on to her children or grandchildren because her native tongue was beaten out of her in residential school fifty years ago.

I ask about her work as an addictions counsellor. She says, "In the work, you don't have emotional ties. You have boundaries. You don't take your stuff home. But when I come home, it's here. I don't like it. I'm getting fed up." I notice worry lines around her eyes and mouth. I know that one of the most important rules with addicts is not to take them into your home to stay with you and their children. That's called enabling. But her daughter had just gotten out of jail, and Ruth said she knew her daughter had no other place to go. That's why she took her in.

Ruth says she took the kids in when she did because she knew they might be abused in a foster or adoptive home, and she was sure they'd be separated from each other. She says she knows she did the right thing, but she's sad about what they lost. She's kept them safe, but "I'm not their mother," she says. "And I lost out on being a grandparent. I'm a grandparent for my son's children, but these ones never had a grandparent." She says, "They have family. I'm their family. Their whole family."

A door hinge squeaks down the hall, followed by soft footsteps: someone barefoot or in moccasins. "This is my granddaughter," Ruth says, as a young woman comes into view. Ruth says to her, "This is the man that's interviewing me." The young woman and I say hi, and I ask her if she wants to say something about what it's been like for her to be raised by her grandmother. She blushes. After pausing to think, she says, "I'd just say it was hard sometimes." I ask what was hard about it. "I'd see my friends, and they could just text their mom." She looks at Ruth. "She doesn't know how to text! And I'd have to turn the TV on for her. Stuff like that."

She chuckles. Ruth says, "But you missed your mother." "No!" the granddaughter says, without a breath of hesitation. I ask her if she felt excluded sometimes at school. "Yeah, a little bit," she mumbles. She looks in the fridge for something to eat, apparently not interested in freshly made moose stew or bannock.

Ruth says, "I myself wouldn't do it again, because I feel everyone loses in the long run. It would be wonderful if the parents would be forced to go and have treatment or cultural training or whatever, to help them get back with their children." She talks about the deep sadness, anger, and resentment she carries because her daughter and the kids' dads were addicts.

The granddaughter leaves to buy ice cream, and Ruth tells me the girl was "a very angry teenager," that she was suicidal when she was 13 and 14 years old. That was when Ruth moved with them to Edmonton, where nobody knew them, and where the granddaughter's classmates wouldn't laugh at her because she had an addicted mother. When Ruth moved back to the reserve six years later, the girl's classmates all had children of their own to raise and they were stuck on the reserve without the chance to make something of their lives. She was sure her granddaughter would have been just like them if they hadn't moved away.

I asked: If drugs were everywhere on reserves, why would teenagers laugh at a classmate for having an addicted mother? Ruth says back then people were ashamed of their addictions and kept them hidden. Now, she says, nobody's ashamed anymore, and you can't even walk down the road without somebody trying to sell you drugs. She says children growing up on the reserve are surrounded by dysfunction. "When they turn eighteen, they go to welfare and they retire. They don't work. They don't want to work. They don't know what work is. No work history. No nothing. It's so sad."

Ruth is certain residential schools are the source of the dysfunction. She testified at the TRC hearings and got counseling, but many others "never worked on their residential school trauma." She was taken from her parents at age 6; the pain of that separation is the main reason she took her grandchildren in, she says, instead of letting them go into the child welfare system. Her husband didn't go to a residential school, but he was an alcoholic, and so her own children grew up in a deeply troubled home. She saw raising the grandchildren as a chance to do it better the second time around.

She tells me that memories of her residential school experience keep coming back and that "healing never stops." She tries to focus primarily on the positive side of the residential school. "My values and morals are very strict from the residential school," she says. "I know you've got to be on time. You gotta live with truth, honesty, forgiveness." I ask her how she learned that at a residential school, and she says, "I didn't want to get brutalized. There were people who did not tell the truth.... They *got it*." She says she was lucky. She concentrated on her studies, and so she wasn't forced to do hard labour. She got a grade 11 education there and, toward the end, she helped other kids with their school work; they'd even pay her 25 cents a lesson!

Her luck goes back at least three generations before her, she says. Her family lived off the land until she was taken away. Her dad was a trapper, hunter, and medicine man; her mother was a gardener. They both farmed. Her dad's dad was a medicine man too, and her dad's grand-father was a chief who signed Treaty 6. "My mom and dad never went to residential school," she says. "When my dad was ten and the residential schools opened, his grandfather took him and went to the trap line." They kept him there and didn't come out because they were scared he'd get taken. Even so, she, like most residen-tial school survivors, turned to alcohol to deal with the trauma, grief, and low self-esteem.

As the interview winds down, Ruth returns to the question I started with: Why did she take in these grand-children? "I wonder how it would have been if I didn't take it to court," she says. "I wonder if she would've smartened up. I don't know. I know through my work a lot of families where children got apprehended, and they made changes and got their children back. Now they have more sup-port for the parents. They have conditions: 'If you don't smarten up by this date…'"

So did Ruth enable her daughter to stay in her addiction when she took the grandkids? "I wonder what would've happened. But I'll never know." She pauses. "I know I won't have any more grandchildren." She pauses again. "But I'm happy they were part of my life. I don't regret it. I'm happy what I did, but I often wonder what could have been the end result if I hadn't been around, because I know I had my heart in there."

At this point my friend, who was in and out of the house during the interview, hands me a pack of Player's cigarettes to give to Ruth. I pass them on to her with my thanks. We say goodbye and get back into the car for the hour-long drive back to town. As we drive east at 110 kilometres an hour, the sun is still high in the sky; it's 5:30 p.m. but we still have five hours of daylight left.

As Ruth moves into the evening of her life, she has one foot in the social services department and one on the reserve. She works in the white world's rules and systems even though she knows they perpetuate calamity and keep centuries-old wounds open. She also knows they offer help that her people need and can't get anywhere else. Ruth's daughter bears the wounds from the residential school system that Ruth passed on to her and the alcoholism Ruth and her husband suffered through when they raised her. Ruth knows that taking her daughter in after she just got out of jail was a way of enabling her and a clear violation of the best practices of her profession. But she loves her daughter and her grandchildren, and her heart tells her that's the right thing to do.

I remember the moose skin stretched out on that board in my friend's garage, held in place by dozens of pins. Ruth is stretched too, to the limit of her strength, torn between conflicting cultures and conflicting demands. But she's alive. The beat of the moose-skin drum is her own heartbeat. The shrill chant of the drummers is her own heartache's prayer to the Creator. The spin and twirl of jingle dancers, the sweet scent of sage smoke spiraling up towards the sun remind her of who she is.

NINE

Dances with Ants

*There's quite a few people who say they're proud of
the way we're raising our grandchildren. I guess
they're always watching or something. We get a lot
of compliments on that. Makes me feel good.*

—*Marcel*

The next day we drove back onto the reserve. All the dirt driveways looked the same. So did all the slender, off-white aspen trunks with their freshly sprouted, golden-green leaf coronas trembling in the spring sun. The cloudless sky was a robin's egg blue. The houses were set back maybe a hundred metres from the road we were on. In rural areas down south, on acreages and farms, people get their mail in roadside mailboxes, but I didn't see any of those here.

My navigator in the passenger seat carried the landscape in his blood and bones, but like a musician picking out a tune he hasn't played in years, he misdirected me and we had to turn around several times. Finally, we pulled up to a field of grass bigger than four substantial suburban lots. A third of it was a golden carpet of dandelions, the rest green grass lush and smooth as a golf course fairway. On the edge of the dandelions, a woman in grey sweats and sunglasses pushed a gas lawnmower, turning the gold into green as she walked. She wiped the sweat off her face with the back of her hand and waved to us.

We parked beside a red Dodge pickup and a minivan. About thirty metres farther on, a Salem Lite trailer sat on the grass with several lawn chairs beside it. A black-and-brown mongrel dog was lying down under it. Off to the right, I saw a homemade wooden outdoor gym floor between two basketball hoops. Two balls were on the grass next to it, as were a black adult-sized bicycle and a red children's bicycle, lying on their sides. Set back well behind the brown and white bungalow, I saw a cabin, another camper trailer, and a screened-in area with a roof on it. Hidden behind some trees, in deep shadow, was another vehicle. A 5-year-old girl laughed and ran toward the basketballs, and a boy and girl who looked about 10 and 12 raced across the grass after her.

My friend introduced me to Donna and Marcel. The skin on Donna's face was deep brown and smooth, with hardly a wrinkle. She could have been 45 or 50. Marcel had a few wrinkles around his eyes, and his jet-black hair was lightly frosted. He was probably in his mid- to late fifties.

Donna, Marcel, and I moved lawn chairs into the shade next to the camper, but my friend decided to sit in the sun a few feet away. I gave Marcel a copy of *Human on the Inside*; I gave Donna a pack of Player's cigarettes. They might not be smokers, but my friend assured me they would appreciate the traditional gift.

"Don't tease the dog!" Donna shouted across the lawn as she raced over to intervene. Marcel told me that in addition to the three children I saw, they also raised Nathan, a 14-year-old grandson, since he was born. Nathan is their oldest son's child. Marcel said he's never felt guilt or shame that the kids' parents couldn't raise them. "I pity the parents, but that doesn't help. They're gonna be the way they wanna be." He told me that, a while ago, the parents lived here in the basement of the bungalow until they got their own place. When they moved, Marcel said, Nathan "didn't want to bother." Nathan stayed with Marcel and Donna until three years ago, when he decided to return to his parents, but he came back after a week. He'd had enough of drinking and fighting. "The mother called the police, eh?" Marcel said with a grin. "They asked Nathan, 'Do you want to live here?' They said he's eleven, and now it's his choice. He's still here. He hunts. I do some hunting too."

Donna rejoined us as Marcel was telling me about Nathan's basketball. "We spend a lot of money just to travel him around for basketball practices and games. He's also a fancy bustle dancer." Donna jumped back up again, ran into the house, and brought back two pictures. One showed a smiling young man in full regalia: green and yellow feathers in long, sweeping fans on both sides, red and blue beadwork in diamond and star patterns on his chest. The other showed an older man, Marcel, in a crowd of several hundred; they were also dressed up in reds, blues, greens, yellows, feathers, beads, fur-trimmed moccasins, headdresses: an explosion of brilliant colours. They both stood on a field of green grass. Above them the sky was a roiling stew of black clouds.

"Oooh, Tyler, be careful!" Donna shouted. The 12-year-old pedaled a bicycle across the yard as the 10-year-old girl clung to the handlebars, her mouth and eyes wide open to the wind.

Shirley, the middle child—"the wild one," as Donna called her—was apprehended with her brother Nathan when she was 2. They were in foster care for six weeks before Donna and Marcel were allowed to see her. "We got her in May," Donna told me, "and kept her until September, when her auntie wanted her. Then in December, her auntie didn't want her anymore." The aunt had applied for the family allowance in September, got it in December, and had a "fantastic Christmas" with her niece before she went back into care. Donna and Marcel were away at the time, and when they came home, Shirley lived with them for three years before going back to her mom again. That's when Nathan went away and came back here a week later.

Shirley stayed with her mom three years and then told the school staff she wanted to live with grandma and grandpa. Donna fought the mother in court for legal custody. Donna said that Shirley's "attitude and behaviour had changed. She's not the girl that left here. She lies. She steals. I have to keep our bedroom door locked because she steals jewelry, money, any shiny object. Because of my job, I go away quite often, for a week at a time." One time, she left $40 so Nathan would have lunch money at school for the week, but then it disappeared. She said that Shirley "took the money to school and started passing it around! She doesn't understand what punishment is, and she can't seem to learn. It's frustrating beyond belief."

Donna said FASD could be part of the problem, but testing for that was still a long way off. She told me she sends her grandkids off reserve for school now because the one close by "has no discipline" and academic standards are low. Nathan went to the reserve school, she said, had behaviour problems, and so she transferred him. "By grade 9, he got As and A+s and one B. He made the gold honour roll!" She hoped Shirley would do better too, but "she's used to going off by herself whenever she wants," Donna said. "When she lived at her mom's, she'd wake up in the morning, get dressed, and go around on her own all day." One night before Shirley lived with them, when she was 8, Donna and Marcel were driving home from Nathan's basketball game when "she goes pedaling by on her bike at 11:30 at night! That's the kind of life she was living. Bringing her back to normal is difficult."

But talking about Nathan is easy for both of them; he's their success story. They drive him to basketball, they travel the powwow dancing circuit with him, and last year they went to Airdrie for the Alberta Summer Games.

Nathan made $3,000 from dancing competitions last year, they said, and he saved most of it.

"For his fourteenth birthday," Marcel said, "I gave him my new rifle, and in November, he killed his first moose."

"By himself!" Donna added. "He was out at the lake. I was out of town. I got a text message saying: 'I got a moose! I got a moose! I got a moose!' He was so excited."

Donna said she gets no financial support, only about $20 a month in family allowances for the boys, because she has a good job. Until she got legal custody of Shirley, it was an informal arrangement. But that caused some problems. When Nathan was in grade 9 and needed vaccinations, the public health nurse wouldn't do them because Donna didn't have legal custody. "So I called the reserve nurse, and she said, 'That's ridiculous. Bring him here and we'll give him his shots.' " But Donna foresaw other, more serious issues, and so got legal custody, "because the white world needs the documents."

Marcel said, "It's okay with the dad, our oldest son, for us to raise these two. He comes to visit now and then."

Suddenly, an eagle appeared above the trees to our right and soared over the house, the yard, all of us. Marcel said, "Hey! Look at that! An eagle! Ha!" We watched it disappear behind the trees to our left and then sat for a moment in silence. Was the Great Spirit blessing this extended family and our conversation? That's what it felt like to me.

Donna said their oldest son wants to take charge of the kids, "but I don't trust him. He's got addictions." The kids' parents live separately, and when the kids visit them, the mom doesn't pay much attention. The 12-year-old boy could be gone all day or even three or four days at a time, and the mother doesn't look for him and never asks him where he went. He seems to drift back and forth between his two parents whenever he feels like it, Donna said. "He's pretty much on his own 24/7. He showed up here last night probably about midnight. Someone knocked on the door, and I jumped. Because no one ever comes here after dark, eh? I go and check the door. He's standing there." She told me his mom lives five miles away from here, with a forest full of cougars and bears in between. "He just shows up here. So he's here for the weekend, I guess. I'm not gonna send him home, because it's safe here. He gets to eat here."

I asked them how they felt about taking on these kids, and whether they think they had much choice about it. Donna said she was angry that her son and his partner wouldn't straighten up and keep their own kids, and she felt forced to take Shirley. But, "instead of these kids disappearing into some other world, I'd rather they stay with me," she said.

Marcel said, "With ours all grown up, it's nice to have little ones." He smiled.

"We had a period of time when it was just us," Donna continued, "and it was really weird. Way too quiet." Marcel laughed long and loud at what was clearly a joke they'd told each other before. Donna said chasing the kids around helps them stay young and fit. "Now we're speaking about it, it's really quiet. I better go check."

While she looked for the kids, Marcel told me it's better for the kids to be here with them because their eldest son doesn't hunt. "So what's he gonna teach his sons?" Marcel said he taught their other two children hunting and trapping, but the eldest simply wasn't interested. "If he picks up moose meat, he's gotta wear gloves!" Marcel laughed. But their daughter, he said, "was cutting hind quarters when she was fourteen."

Donna sat down again, and we talked about the parents' addictions. She said their ex-daughter-in-law was probably addicted since she was 13; by 18 she had two children. When her son started the relationship, the maternal grandmother was already raising those two kids, one of which was 6 years old at the time.

At this point in the conversation, all four kids cut across in front of us and stop to show us their trophy: a 2-litre clear plastic pop bottle with about ten bees buzzing around inside. Then they giggle, shriek, and run off again, probably in search of other prey. Donna and Marcel shrug.

Donna told me their son went to high school in Edmonton. When he came home, he was addicted too. She said addiction—everything from prescription drugs to crystal meth—is common on the reserve. I asked what she thought the underlying cause might be. She said everyone points to residential schools, but she's not convinced that is the single reason, as so many more injustices have occurred in the second and third generations since the schools closed. Raising her grandchildren was something she could do to help, Donna said, but she had no idea how to help the larger community. The welfare director tried making social assistance clients attend information sessions about addiction, but that didn't help. Marcel suggested social services should help people find jobs, "instead of just handing a cheque over." He blamed the band leadership for doing nothing about drugs and alcohol, and he said banning alcohol on the reserve would be a good place to start.

In the inner-city neighbourhood where I live, neighbours keep an eye on each other's houses, talk to each other on the sidewalks, and sometimes organize potluck socials. I assumed that on the reserve, where almost everybody is related to everybody else, Donna and Marcel would get at least a little support from neighbours. But they said that, except for Donna's sister, nobody on the reserve helps them at all. Donna told me that because of "judgment and opinions and clanship, backstabbing, gossip," she and Marcel don't even associate with people on the reserve: "It's not a nice place." Marcel said, "We're happy to leave here on the weekend, as long as the house is safe." During the week, "we're gone in the morning and not back till five."

For them, the powwows are a deeply spiritual experience, part of their cultural heritage, a practice "that holds everything together." Their daily smudging ceremony at home keeps them connected to each other and to where they came from. But they said there's almost nobody on the reserve they would trust with their grandchildren if the two of them ever had to be away at the same time.

"Thankfully," Donna said, "that hasn't happened." If it did, her first choice would be families that honour Indigenous culture and spirituality—not people on this reserve, but people they know from the powwow trail.

As our conversation ended, I asked Donna and Marcel if they'd like to add anything. Donna said, "I think anybody going into this for the first time should think about the statement that it only takes one person to care to change someone's life." Her voice broke as she stifled a sob; tears formed in her eyes, and she struggled to hold them back. "I think"—she took a deep breath—"that's what got me." Her voice wavered. "Because I had to save her! I couldn't just watch what was happening!"

As my friend and I walked to the car to leave, I looked around. I recalled something Marcel said. Thirty years ago, when he and Donna hadn't been married very long, they came here to build a house. "All this was nothing but trees," he said. "I told her, since we're getting the house, let's walk around. It was spring, eh? There was snow here and there. I told her, 'Look for a spot where there's ants. That's the place it'll melt first.'"

I looked at the house and wondered, was this some traditional teaching? Did he have personal experience building on a flood plain? Where did he learn to observe even the smallest wildlife? Wherever it came from, this wisdom felt like something he learned from his father, grandmother, or an Elder. It seemed counterintuitive to me. Shouldn't a person avoid building on an anthill? Wouldn't their house be infested with ants?

But they built the house where the ants were and decided to live with the ants. When the first flood came, the water rose up to the bumper of that truck in the driveway, Marcel said, but the house was safe on dry land, an island in a sea of troubles, the eye of a hurricane. A storm of addiction, poverty, and other fallout from the residential school era inspired Donna and Marcel to dance with tears and laughter, to dance with rain clouds, with little children, with bees and basketballs, and yes, even with ants.

Marcel and his grandson dance in full regalia all along the powwow circuit every summer. Marcel and Donna and their grandchildren dance every day of their lives in ordinary clothing. That's how intergenerational relationships like theirs work: the grandparents decide to connect with each other and with the children as dance partners. Sometimes they're out of sync, sometimes they step on each other's feet, and sometimes they simply have to find different music.

This type of dance involves using our heads as well as our hearts and feet. In fact, I would argue that interactions with other people should engage all our brain cells and all the neurons in every part of our bodies.

TEN

A Three-Generation Brain Dance

*All of imagination—everything we think,
we feel, we sense—comes through the human
brain. And once we create new patterns in
this brain, once we shape the brain in a new
way, it never returns to its original shape.*
—*Jay S. Walker*

Consider this fictionalized scenario.

A 50-year-old father yells at his 17-year-old son, Tim, "What were you *thinking*?" He's just found out he's going to be a grandfather, and he's not happy. "Why didn't you at least use a condom?"

Tim stares down at his shoes: Nike Air All-Sport runners. He got them three months ago and wore them when he took Cindy to see *The Fault in Our Stars* at the Princess Theatre. He held her hand all through the movie. He squeezed it when Hazel took off her bra in that Amsterdam hotel room and she and Gus made love for the first time.

He glanced over at Cindy and saw her look back at him. He blushed and turned toward the screen.

As he remembers that night, blood rushes to his penis, just like at the Princess. It gets harder, presses against the front of his boxers and pushes the stiff, quadruple-reinforced zipper seams of his blue jeans out into a bulge. He's back in Cindy's basement after the movie. Cindy's tongue strokes his lips. His tongue stretches out to meet hers. His heart beats faster. His penis gets stiffer. His hand inside her blouse, under her bra, he caresses her nipple between his thumb and forefinger until it's a firm little nub. Then it's his bare chest against hers, her smooth, perfect skin like the soft topside of a cloud. Her legs spread apart, then flex, lift with every thrust of his pelvis, faster, faster, faster…and into hyperdrive until the Milky Way, Andromeda, and a cluster of nameless galaxies spurt past in a blur.

He wakes up afterwards with his head on her shoulder. The Earth is still far beneath them. He closes his eyes again. His skin caresses hers head to toe, one leg across her thigh, one arm across her chest. They drift out past the edge of time, beyond space, beyond darkness. Tim-and-Cindy. Tim-Cindy. TimCindyCindyTim. Nowalways. Alwaysnow….

When he should be responding to his father's question, Tim's brain recreates the whole experience in a fraction of a second, long enough to make his father even madder. "What were you *THINKING*???" His father yells even louder.

In family courts across the Western world, every day they're in session, children's names are on the dockets by the thousands. Biological mothers, fathers, aunts, uncles, grandmothers, grandfathers, great-grandparents, lawyers, social workers, hockey coaches, elementary schoolteachers, friends, neighbours, psychologists, pastors, stenographer, clerk, and judge gather to decide: What next? What next for children whose mother and father conceived them without thinking? Whose mother and father knew too well how to start a child but too little how to parent one?

If Tim's father had asked, "Why didn't you use your head?" Tim could have answered honestly, "But I did!" The human brain contains more synapses than there are stars in the universe; thinking is only one of many things it does. The brain flexes the lower leg when a doctor taps just below the kneecap with a rubber hammer. It tells the heart and lungs when to pump and breathe. It directs a rush of blood to the penis when sexual intercourse is in sight.

In *Stiffed: The Betrayal of the American Man*, Susan Faludi talks about a male porn star who made it big because he could maintain an erection longer than anyone else, and could have a second erection after ejaculation more quickly than anyone else. Her chapter title, "Waiting for Wood," refers to what the crew does on the set after male climax. When the penis gets stiff as wood again, they can start to shoot the next scene. In some hard-core sex scenes, Faludi says, penises are the stars, and the men are simply the penises' life support systems. The industry measures the quality of penises by their size when they're hard but also by how hard they are. A high-quality penis is hard as a piece of wood and just about as smart.[1]

When 17-year-old Tim let his penis overrule his still maturing prefrontal cortex in the scenario described above, he and Cindy created a lifelong stream of difficulties for themselves, for their parents, for the child they conceived, for taxpayers and social workers. Males much older than Tim have let their penises wreak havoc too. US president Bill Clinton was impeached and nearly forced from office because he let his penis make decisions for him. Clinton is only one in a long line of politicians, priests, coaches, and husbands who were defrocked, disgraced, and divorced— all because of "wood."

An intelligent life form from outside our solar system who observed family court proceedings would surely laugh at the insanity of it: Earthlings make a person pass a written test and a road test before he or she can legally drive a car, but they allow each other to make a new human being on a whim. Earthlings have no rules about this until the child is born and gets a birth certificate. Conceiving a child is the most common do-it-yourself project in the world. Governments get involved at various points along the way. In Canada it goes like this. Under the authority of Her Majesty the Queen's royal seal, our provincial governments certify: yes, this is a human baby, born on this date, at this place and time; this is its name, and these are its parents. The law says that if anyone witnesses this baby

---

1   Susan Faludi, *Stiffed: The Betrayal of the American Man* (New York: Harper Collins, 1999).

being abused or neglected, they are obliged to report it. But we have no laws to prevent abusive, negligent parents from conceiving more children for grandparents, foster parents, and social workers to take care of.

Brains are made of soft tissue, of course, not wood. Genitalia are too. Brains and genitalia connect to each other through a complex network of neurons. In fact, every part of the human body is saturated with neurons. Over 60 per cent of the cells in the human heart are neurons, and genitalia, skin, intestines—every part of us—has plenty of neurons too. Dr. Norman Doidge estimates we have a hundred million neurons in our gut alone.[2] We are wired to survive. Tim and Cindy's attraction to each other is part of their will to survive. They defend themselves against danger—an attack by an angry parent or a hungry bear, for example—by the three Fs: fight, flight, or freeze. They defend themselves against the certainty of death by generating new life. That's how the dinosaurs survived for millions of years. Stegosauruses as big as houses lived full lives even though their brains were the size of walnuts.[3] Those lizard brains were all dinosaurs needed to rule the Earth for about 150 million years.

Human beings have lizard brains too; they're called the brain stem and cerebellum. We're a "higher" life form, not because we drink alcohol and take drugs, but

---

2   See Doidge's *The Brain's Way of Healing* (New York: Penguin, 2015), xviii.
3   I remember this from Bertha Morris Parker's *The New Golden Treasury of Natural History*, which was, when I was growing up, the equivalent of having a know-it-all scientist living in my bedroom.

because our brains are more complex. Our lizard brain is like the foundation of a house; the other parts are where we think and feel and live our lives, but without the foundation, we die. If we drink too much, sense we're under threat, or get sexually aroused, our inner stegosaurus takes over.

The lizard brain was the most intelligent brain on Earth for about 400 million years.[4] About 150 million years ago the limbic brain (a.k.a. the midbrain) was born when the first small mammals arrived. Warm-blooded animals—cats, mastodons, mice, and goats, for example—developed the capacity to remember experiences that gave them pleasure or pain, or scared them and enabled them to avoid or repeat similar experiences.

Our limbic system is where we experience emotions. If we have a gut feeling about something, that's our limbic system. We don't have to think about it or decide to feel it: it just happens. When Tim's father found out Tim got Cindy pregnant, his limbic brain remembered teenagers he knew whose lives got derailed by pregnancy. He remembered close calls he had himself. He didn't think; his limbic system did what it's supposed to do. It reacted.

The third part of the brain, the cerebral cortex or neocortex, became significant as primates evolved, between two and three million years ago. This is by far the largest

---

4   For more on the lizard brain, see http://thebrain.mcgill.ca/flash/d/d_05/d_05_cr/d_05_cr_her/d_05_cr_her.html, and Michael Mendizza, *Magical Parent, Magical Child: The Art of Joyful Parenting* (Berkeley, CA: North Atlantic Books, 2004), 15.

part of the human brain. The neocortex is extremely flexible, which gives it a nearly unlimited capacity to learn. Our self-talk happens here: we reason things out, anticipate and imagine the future, and make conscious decisions instead of simply acting from the gut. The neocortex is not fully developed until we're in our twenties, which is why the US Supreme Court, in *Roper v. Simmons* (2005), ruled it is unconstitutional to execute someone under 18. The psychiatric community in the United States convinced the court that before their neocortex is developed, young people don't have the capacity to understand the consequences of their actions, and the justices decided it is wrong to electrocute or lethally inject someone if that person's brain isn't mature enough.[5]

In the interminable abortion debate, I've heard arguments that the one-celled zygote constitutes human life and should be protected by law. I've also heard that until a child is a mature adult—say, at age 25—he or she isn't fully human and shouldn't have human rights.[6] Our neocortex keeps maturing for twenty-some years after birth, even though other systems in the body, like the reproductive system, mature much earlier. In Tim and Cindy's case, that would be seven or eight years before their neocortices have the ability to make good decisions about using their genitalia.

---

5   People with FASD and other brain injuries may also lack the capacity to understand cause and effect, depending on the severity of the condition.

6   A similar argument has been used throughout human history to justify racism, eugenics, enslavement, war, misogyny, and a host of other evils.

While Tim's and Cindy's frontal lobes are still developing, Tim's sperm meets Cindy's egg. After that, Cindy's lizard brain keeps adjusting her hormone levels to feed the consequences of their action. Tim's father shames him, which Tim shares with Cindy—if their parents still let them talk to each other at all. Meanwhile, Cindy's parents shame her too. This makes her tense, sad, angry, et cetera, and upsets her natural hormone balance and her usual good humour. These external events alter her body chemistry beyond what the pregnancy has already done, while The Consequence—who I'll call Connie for short—lives and grows in the constantly changing stew of Cindy's hormones, electrochemical currents, increased blood pressure and heart rate. Cindy's body chemistry directly affects the structure and chemistry of Connie's brain. Even the angry voices of Connie's grandparents and Tim's tears and groans have an impact on that brain as it grows.

On the plus side, Cindy doesn't have to think about when to tack on arms and legs, when to start up Connie's heart, whether Connie will be a boy, girl, or transgendered person, or which neurons to connect to which muscles. It's not like she's building a Lego fort or a Tinkertoy Ferris wheel. The genetic material she and Tim so enthusiastically contributed contains the design and the drive to develop *itself* into a baby.

As Connie develops, her brain grows from the inside out, just like evolution happening all over again. The lizard brain comes first, then the midbrain, then the cerebral cortex. During the peak brain-formation period, up to 250,000 neurons are added per minute. At birth, Connie will have about 100 billion neurons,[7] As the baby grows, each neuron sprouts extensions called dendrites to receive signals from other neurons. Each neuron grows extensions called axons that send those signals. The place where one cell's axon touches another cell's dendrite is called a synapse. A synapse is like the best-known bit of *The Creation of Adam* on the Sistine Chapel ceiling, in which Michelangelo has an old man with a beard representing God, who extends his index finger to touch Adam's index finger and bring him to life. The neuron's life work is to connect with other neurons. Neurons are extreme extroverts that come alive when they're engaged with others. Dr. Daniel Amen estimates that each neuron could have up to 40,000 connections with other neurons. One hundred billion neurons multiplied by 40,000 connections—that's a number exponentially bigger than the US national debt![8]

Like all healthy extroverts, neurons make many connections, and they use some more than others. Some they use all the time, like the ones to pump blood and inflate lungs. Some they stop using, like the ones that remember Tim's previous girlfriends' telephone numbers; these get dropped. Axons that get used a lot develop a coating of myelin, which works like insulation on a wire. The brain's

---

7   *Making a Good Brain Great* (New York: Three Rivers Press, 2005), 21. I am indebted to Dr. Daniel Amen for much of the technical information in this section, which I have paraphrased and to which I've added my own gloss.

8   Amen, *Making a Good Brain Great*, 20.

electrochemical impulses travel ten times faster along a heavily myelinated axon than they do along an axon without myelin. When Connie hears Cindy's mother bang a frying pan against the kitchen counter and shriek, "If you don't abort that baby, you'll get no money from us!" Connie's brain develops more efficient connections for defence—fight, flight, or freeze—and fewer for pleasure and rational thought, for example.

Scientists say that as a human brain develops, starting in the womb, it prunes off unused connections. This happens in a preteen who isn't learning a second language, and the ability to learn new languages declines as a result. A grandmother loses her memory if she doesn't use it. When the brain is alive, pulsating with activity, it's like a delicate, intricate spider web suspended in clear fluid. Dr. Amen says that suspension's viscosity is somewhere between egg whites and Jell-O.[9] The brain is very unlike a computer with wires, motherboards, memory chips, and cooling fans. But a parent lying awake in bed at 2:00 a.m., waiting, hyper-alert, for a teenager to come home from a date, imagining an unintended pregnancy or a fatal car crash over and over, might as well be trapped in a wire loop or on a train traveling a circular track.

Copper wires, steel rails, pruning, spider web, Jell-O. The brain is none of these, and it's not made of plastic either, even though neuroscience's most significant recent discovery has been neuroplasticity. Until the 1990s, the

---

9 Amen, *Making a Good Brain Great*, 24.

consensus was that after about age 20, the brain toboganed downhill toward senility, neurons dying by hundreds of thousands every day, even without the help of alcohol or drugs. Anybody over 60 trying to learn a new language, play a musical instrument, or take up dancing knows it's like swimming upstream in a river. I never played the guitar until I took lessons in 2004, when I was 55. My 55-year-old fingers needed many more repetitions than the 20-year-old fingers in my class to play clear D or G chords. But I did it, even though I was definitely an old dog already.

Before I heard about brain plasticity, an even older dog—my dad—showed me how he kept his mind sharp through exercise. He was a stubborn old cuss. He'd focus on something, set a goal, and just do it. In his late eighties, he decided to avoid two common hazards of old age: wheelchairs and dementia. At least an hour each day he'd sit in a chair and do modified leg lifts, he'd stretch his hamstrings and quads, and he'd take walks. When he died at 92, he had no wheelchair and had never fallen.

His brain exercise was too daunting for me to try even though I was thirty years younger. Several times I visited him, and he asked me to write one hundred random words in columns on a sheet of lined paper and to number them. Then he studied the list for an hour or two. He gave it back to me and asked me to quiz him. In fact, he pushed it across the dining room table with his lips pursed, his eyes squinched tight as if he were golfing in Arizona sunshine without sunglasses. He was proud of his memory and fiercely competitive. He'd sit on the front edge of his chair, lean forward, and lock eyes with me like a batter at home plate daring a pitcher to try to get one by him. And he didn't want to recite the words in order and have me check his answers; he'd ask me to jump around, to challenge him, to ask, "What's 73? What's 46? 87?" He usually missed three or four, and he winced at each of his failures. But I was amazed how many he got right. I wasn't anywhere close to that good at remembering people's names or lines of poetry, even in my thirties.

Neural plasticity applies to seriously injured brains too. In *The Brain that Changes Itself*, Dr. Norman Doidge tells of a university professor who has a massive stroke. The experts give up on him, but his son decides to teach him to crawl, as if he were a baby. That tiny step starts the dad's recovery and he's eventually able to resume his career. Dr. Doidge also tells of a woman born with an entire brain hemisphere missing. One-half of her cranial cavity had no brain tissue in it, but the half brain she did have developed twice the normal connections, and she lived a normal life.[10]

If Cindy and Tim were binge drinkers and not binge lovers, Connie's growing prenatal brain would face more serious problems than her grandmother's shrieks and her mother's worries. She could develop the thin upper lip, smooth philtrum,[11] and narrow eyes of an FASD child.

---

10 See *The Brain that Changes Itself: Stories of Personal Triumph from the Frontiers of Brain Science* (New York: Penguin, 2007).

11 The philtrum is the vertical groove directly under the centre of the nose.

Her brain could develop dead zones, depending on what parts of her brain were forming when her mother drank. Connie might struggle to master basic reading skills, or suffer from extreme mood swings. She might be diagnosed with ADHD or ODD. If Cindy were a drug addict, Connie could be born addicted to crack cocaine, heroin, or crystal meth, with all the distortions to brain development that would entail. If Cindy and Tim were poor and didn't have enough to eat, had to sleep outside under a tree in the cold, lived in refugee camps or war zones, or if they abused or neglected Connie, Connie would have serious neurological issues and maybe other chronic physical problems too.

Consider another possibility: What if Tim and Cindy can't take the stress and break up? What if neither of them wants to invest the time, money, or energy needed to raise Connie? They might put Connie up for adoption so they can finish growing up. They might ask Connie's grandparents to take her in and be her parents; in that case, Tim and Cindy could become like grandparents to Connie, visiting her when they want to but otherwise living child-free.

When Tim's father yelled at him at the start of this chapter, he joined a long tradition of fathers disappointed in their children, starting with God Almighty in *Genesis* and immortalized in literature: Shakespeare's Romeo and Juliet, Ovid's Pyramus and Thisbe, and Chava and Fyedka from *Fiddler on the Roof*, to name just a few well-known examples. After the shock wore off, Tim's father and mother might think about taking in Baby Connie, with or without her parents. As they do that, here's a summary of what's likely happening in the seven brains involved in this three-generation community during the pregnancy.

We have two aging grandparent brains in Cindy's house and two more in Tim's. All four struggle with shame and anxiety, which colours their thinking and all their actions. They have four brains becoming less efficient by the day simply because of aging, brains pruned to facilitate repeating neurological activity and discourage new connections, memories that are less and less efficient. Their older brains are most likely suited to live in a slower-moving, less computerized, more private, more black-and-white world. In the next generation, Tim and Cindy's, we have two active reproductive systems, two adolescent brains with still-growing neocortices posting Instagram photos of Cindy's expanding waistline and of the latest embryo ultrasound. Finally, we have one embryonic brain making billions of new cells and connections by the hour, adjusting to Cindy's moods and chemistry and responding to the sounds of the outside world.

Human beings have proportionately larger brains than any other animal, but if grandparenting or parenting were only about brains and thinking, *Homo sapiens* would be a very different species. Each of us would be like a stereotypical extraterrestrial being from an old black-and-white sci-fi movie: head twice as big as the body, an alien thing that is merely a life-support system for a brain. If Tim and Cindy's parents were only *thinking*, they'd never consider taking in a new baby, with or without its parents. It doesn't make sense. It's not rational. Cindy and Tim weren't thinking when they fell in love and had sex, but grandparents who take in grandkids to raise aren't using their heads either. Anybody who says *Homo sapiens* evolved as we did and put ourselves on top of the food chain just because bigger brains are better is missing the point. Every grandparent I've met who's taken in a grandchild did it because of love. And one person can only love another if his/her neocortex is mature and if, back in early childhood, he/she developed a healthy attachment that would be the foundation for all future relationships.

Cindy and Tim's parents spent seventeen years developing their attachment to Cindy and Tim. Cindy and Tim spent maybe two years attaching to each other before they conceived Connie. For Cindy and Tim "going all the way" meant genital intercourse. If their neocortices had been more mature, they would have realized "going all the way" means feeding Connie and changing her diapers at 3:00 a.m. It means helping her learn to read, consoling her after she falls off her bike or skins her knee, drying her tears over teenage crushes and breakups, or counseling her through career-selection nail-biting. It means handholding, advising, helping Connie with marriage plans and being there when she has her own children. It means taking in Connie's children when Connie needs a break. It could even mean Cindy and Tim using the brain cells in their hearts and the neurons in their mature neocortices and taking those grandchildren into their home if Connie can't raise them. It means taking their places as a link in the chain of generations going back to the first cave couple a million years ago and moving forward for as long as the species survives.

For grandparents to raise grandchildren who have healthy brains is one thing; to raise grandchildren with traumatized or malformed brains is an entirely different experience. Indeed, one of the most insidious brain injuries grandparents have to deal with is what results from prenatal exposure to alcohol.

ELEVEN

Raising a Skipped-Generation
FASD Child

*Teratogen: an agent or factor that causes
the malformation of an embryo.*
—New Oxford American Dictionary

Elly holds up a two-inch-high, red plastic capital D. She asks her 6-year-old grandchild, "What does this letter say, Suzie?" Suzie looks at it for half a second, hops down from her chair, and runs away from the dining room table into the adjacent living room. She hops on one foot, then the other. She slowly draws her right hand, then her left, across her eyes like she saw a belly dancer do at a festival last weekend. She swivels her hips to the beat of a song playing inside her head.

"*Suzie*," Elly croons, as sweetly as she can—she's had plenty of practice. "I know you've been studying this letter all week in school. I *know* you know it. Please come back to the table and tell me what this letter says. What sound does it make?"

Suzie drops her arms to her side. She looks down at her feet, which slide as slowly as slugs across the linoleum floor. When she gets close to the table, she looks up at the D again, plops her bum onto the floor, and sobs. "I don't know, Grandma! *I don't know!*" Elly pulls Suzie onto her lap and puts her arms around her. "Why am I so *stupid?*" Suzie whimpers.

During the check-in at her monthly support group meeting, Elly tells a group of foster parents, adoptive parents, and social workers, "We have funding for a tutor for Suzie. Children's Services will cover it. But the tutor who's made great progress with Suzie can only come during school hours. So I talked to Suzie's grade 2 teacher. She said the school has space for tutors to work with students during school hours. They're doing it for other kids. She was happy Suzie would get the help she needs but said we'd need the principal's approval." Elly's voice turns angry. Tears form in her eyes. "I couldn't believe what the principal said! She said Suzie 'might just be a little slow'! The principal said we should see how Suzie does by the end of the year. And when I told her we think Suzie might have FASD—I still can't believe it, she said, 'Well, if Suzie has FASD, she might never learn to read, and tutoring would be a waste of time.' "

A foster mother across the room says, "Yeah, those people can be so ignorant! Why doesn't the Department of Education have programs to make sure principals and teachers know about FASD? It's sure a big enough problem."

"But not all of them are ignorant," an adoptive mother says. "We found a teacher who's been really great with Kylie."

A few others share their experiences with schools, some positive, some negative. The social worker chairing the meeting says, "There's so much inconsistency out there. But there's hope it will improve soon. Premier Redford surprised everybody when, in one of her first statements since she became premier, she said confronting FASD would be one of her top priorities. It's too soon to say what that means, but to have a premier give FASD that kind of attention can only be good."[1]

As I write this, I note that Alberta is on its third premier since Alison Redford left office, even though that was only two years ago. I note, too, that in Edmonton, where I live, the Glenrose Rehabilitation Hospital's diagnostic clinic has a waiting list of over two years. This waiting list is only for children whose mother has been formally documented drinking during pregnancy. The Glenrose clinic is the only place in the Edmonton region where Alberta Health Care will cover the cost. It's possible to get a diagnosis privately and pay for it yourself, but the cost is prohibitive.[2]

---

1 Alison Redford became premier of Alberta in October 2011 when she won the Progressive Conservative leadership race. She led the Conservatives to victory in the April 2012 election, but was forced to resign in March 2014 when she lost the support of her party. Despite her stated commitment to making FASD a priority, she did not manage to make progress on the issue during her short time in office.

2 Egon Johnsson, Liz Dennett, and Gail Littlejohn, eds., *Fetal Alcohol... (continued)*

An Indigenous man I met in Ontario who, with his wife, is raising three children with FASD, told me that when he took them to Toronto for testing, the cost was about $30,000 each. Luckily for him, his band's health unit covered it. Even so, because his family lived over two hours' drive away, they had to spend three weeks away from home in order to take the kids through this complex and time-consuming process.

Provincial health-care systems have very good financial reasons to be careful about what diagnostic procedures they cover. If every child suspected of having some degree of FASD were diagnosed, the cost would be astronomical. One expert in the field estimates the incidence of FASD is between 2 and 9 per 1,000 births, and that the prevalence of FASD in the overall population is between 25 and 233 per 1,000 people. (The range is so broad because of inconsistencies in the reporting across jurisdictions.) Another expert, Philip May, says the damage caused by drinking during pregnancy has been seriously underestimated. He says that "in the United States and Canada, and especially Europe, between fifteen and thirty percent of all kids have been exposed to a significant amount of alcohol as fetuses."[3]

To attach an official FASD diagnosis to a child seems to many caregivers as expensive and difficult as getting a

---

...*Spectrum Disorder (FASD): Across the Lifespan, Proceedings from an IHE Consensus Development Conference 2009* (Edmonton: Institute of Health Economics, 2009), 17.

3   Cited in Johnston, *Drink*, 129.

PhD. To be sure, there are significant benefits. The child could get a lifetime disability pension if the damage is severe. The child could get a classroom aide in school and qualify for special programs. Caregivers would have a better understanding of why their child behaves the way he or she does. Doctors would know how to modify the diagnosis and treatment of other health issues that arise. But like many labels, FASD is a stigma, a red flag that tells others, "This child is defective, abnormal. Stay away!"

So knowledgeable caregivers who suspect that their child has FASD usually spend time deciding whether battling for a diagnosis is worth the trouble. When I observed some meetings of Coaching Families,[4] the emphasis was primarily on understanding the complexity of FASD, the many ways it presents itself, and how to help an FASD child. Getting an official diagnosis was a low priority for the group's members because diagnoses are so hard to come by. Most of the people I've talked to simply resort to informal, do-it-yourself guesswork.

Heavy alcohol consumption during pregnancy can have a profound and visible effect. The damage can be much more than trouble learning to read, difficulty concentrating, inability to understand the connection between actions and consequences, or problems regulating emotions. A 1992 article in *National Geographic* illustrated what happened when a woman drank a quart of vodka a day until she found out she was two months pregnant.

---

4   Coaching Families is a support group in Edmonton for caregivers of children with suspected FASD.

Her son's many disabilities included small, wide-set eyes, damaged corneas, drooping eyelids, malfunctioning kidneys and stomach, a smaller than normal head, a thin upper lip, a short, upturned nose, and a receding chin. He was undersized at birth, and at the age of 3, he was barely starting to talk.[5]

When a woman drinks during pregnancy, the alcohol could radically damage her child's brain, and that damage is permanent. At conception, a child might have the potential to be the next Albert Einstein or Marie Curie. Add alcohol to the pregnancy at a critical time, and that potential could be lost. Some experts say just a couple of drinks at day nineteen or twenty of the pregnancy can cause serious damage, but it's almost impossible, except in extreme cases, to prove the connection between the ensuing damage and a specific instance of drinking. Too many other factors are involved: nutrition, the mother's physical and emotional condition, social setting, and more.

At a public FASD information session at the downtown branch of the Edmonton Public Library, I heard Dr. Gail Andrews talk about her work at the FASD diagnostic clinic at the Glenrose Hospital. She said it's not unusual for a mother whose FASD baby has been taken away to have a second, third, or fourth, hoping that eventually she can keep one. I went to a policy forum at which Alberta Children's Services asked social workers, foster parents, and other caregivers for suggestions on how to address

5   George Steinmetz, "Fetal Alcohol Syndrome," *National Geographic* 191, no. 2 (February 1992), 36–9.

the problems of children in care, particularly FASD children. A long-time foster mother said, "I know this is politically incorrect and that I'm going to sound like Hitler. But wouldn't it be better for everyone if we sterilized women who keep having more babies, when we know the babies will be damaged in utero and end up wards of the province? If we don't, we'll keep enabling these women, costing the public more money, and burdening the caregivers." The room immediately erupted in applause. But despite that support, given the recent history of eugenics in Alberta and elsewhere, no political party would dare adopt the practice.[6]

I've met many grandparents who raise grandchildren and face a dilemma that, in effect, goes like this: "If my addicted son/daughter has another child who gets apprehended, will I take that one in too?" It's an agonizing choice. Some simply say no, but all of them consider taking in one more even though they are already stretching the limit of what they can do. Even to raise one FASD child would challenge the most experienced, knowledgeable,

---

6 The case of Leilani Muir brought Alberta's long-standing practice of eugenics into the public eye when, in 1996, she successfully sued the government for wrongfully sterilizing her at the Provincial Training School for Mental Defectives in Red Deer in 1959. Her story is the subject of a 1996 National Film Board of Canada documentary, *The Sterilization of Leilani Muir* (directed by Glynis Whiting). In "Eugenics: Keeping Canada Sane," the *Canadian Encyclopedia* notes that the 1928 Alberta Sexual Sterilization Act created the Alberta Eugenics Board, which sterilized 2,822 people before it was abolished in 1972 (see http://www.thecanadianencyclopedia.ca/en/article/eugenics-keeping-canada-sane-feature/). Of course, the most notorious instance of mass eugenics occurred under Adolph Hitler and included efforts to exterminate Jews, gypsies, and others by the millions.

skilled, and loving grandparent. But Maria Montanero somehow survived. She shared with me her experience raising an adopted daughter and a granddaughter, both with FASD.

When I met Maria at her split-level home in suburban Edmonton, it was a warm September morning. Maria opened the door and apologized for the mess her house was in; she hoped I wouldn't mind. I looked around and saw not one speck of dust on her glass-topped coffee table or her shining, new-looking hardwood floors, not one smudge on any of the windows that let in the glorious fall sunshine.

Before I came, I knew Maria had raised a 16-year-old granddaughter with FASD, and I wanted to hear about Maria's experience first-hand. She showed me a picture: a dark-haired girl in a blue dress with bright eyes and an engaging smile. She showed me a picture of what the same girl looked like twenty years older. She said the second one was her daughter, Dorothea, now 38 years old and pregnant with her second child. She's married now and lives with her husband and Daniella, the teenager Maria raised.

Maria and her husband came to Canada from South America about forty years ago. They had no children but wanted to adopt two from their old country, "because my heart was always with the street kids," she said. They went there and started the international adoption process with a foster home and brought back with them two children unrelated to each other: Dorothea, who was about 5 then, and baby Miguel. Dorothea's age was a guess; they had no documentation. "She seemed very smart, very bright, with a lot of energy," Maria said.

Maria and her husband, Manuel, arrived at Edmonton International Airport at 11:00 p.m. on Christmas Eve eager to begin their new life with Dorothea and Miguel. They imagined their future as a Christmas present waiting to be opened, but they soon faced challenges. School was the first hurdle. Other children Dorothea's age were already halfway through kindergarten. Dorothea didn't know a word of English and, Maria said, "was never taught anything." She didn't have any of the simple skills her classmates had, like colouring. Maria, a teacher herself, decided to teach Dorothea at home before she sent her to school, to make it less difficult for her. "She caught on very easily," Maria said. "I taught her the alphabet in English. Wow! She caught on so fast! I knew she was smart."

Maria told me very little of Miguel, but the contrast between the two was stark. Miguel learned to read before even going to kindergarten because he observed the lessons Maria gave Dorothea. He showed no symptoms of FASD, was an honours student through school, and has lived a normal life. "Dorothea's behaviour was different," Maria said. "She was very attached to all the guys, whether it was a little boy or a man. I knew she had been in a foster home. There was a dad and a mom there. I couldn't understand that." She worried that something was wrong.

Maria told me Dorothea hugged the boys' and men's legs and always wanted the older men to pick her up and hold her. She would say hi to women and other girls but was shy and reserved with them. With boys and men, she had no boundaries. Maria never found any evidence of sexual abuse. And sure enough, when Dorothea's daughter Danielle was little, Maria noticed the same pattern of behaviour. Maria was with Danielle since she was born, she said, and she knows for certain that Danielle was never abused. When she asked Dorothea about life in the foster home, Dorothea said the foster father was never home. Still, Maria wondered what this behaviour could mean. She was sure it meant something.

As Dorothea was growing up, she struggled to focus on anything. She couldn't sit still at the dining room table. "Dinnertime was a disaster," Maria said. She'd see things on the other side of the room that she wanted to look at, pick up and play with instead of eating her food. She'd squirm in her chair, get down, go somewhere else, come back. A psychologist suggested they put a clock in front of her so Dorothea would know exactly how long she'd have to spend at the table. Another psychologist said that since she likes soup so much, why not buy a bowl that has flowers painted on the inside; she'll be fascinated watching the flowers appear as she eats. They thought she had ADHD. They followed the psychologist's advice, but the flowery bowl didn't make much difference.

When Dorothea was in grade 5, Maria got a call from her teacher: Dorothea was disrupting the class. Maria came in and observed Dorothea and saw her move constantly from desk to desk. Sometimes she'd just stand next to another student's desk. The teachers thought Dorothea had "attitude." They said she'd be in the resource room but wouldn't let anybody help her. Maria was sure it was a learning disability like dyslexia. A psychologist thought it wasn't ADHD but wasn't sure what it was. Maria had no information about Dorothea's parents. She didn't know what FASD was until later.

The daily struggle continued. Then Dorothea turned sixteen and demanded to know about her biological parents. She insisted on going back to see the foster home in South America. Maria was certain the foster home wouldn't tell her anything, but Dorothea was so persistent that they took her. They were surprised the foster mother would even see them, but in the end she didn't say much. She said Dorothea was found abandoned in the city, turned in to the police, and nobody knew who her parents were, only that they were drug addicts and alcoholics who lived on the street.

Maria said hearing that further traumatized Dorothea, and after they returned to Canada, she ran away from home. Dorothea came back five years later. She was pregnant, but she didn't tell them. She lied that she only needed a place for a little while, lied that she was getting a job. Maria said she often came home drunk and lied about that too. When Maria saw she was drinking and pregnant, Maria confronted her: "You're doing to your daughter the same thing your mom did to you!" Dorothea said, "Oh, no. It's not gonna happen. My friend says the baby is used to it." When Danielle was born, Maria prayed she didn't have FASD. Dorothea's pediatrician didn't find any evidence of it. He noted that neither mother nor daughter has FASD facial features.

Danielle was smart and learned quickly. She was in an academic program until grade 3, but had to switch into the regular program when she lost the ability to concentrate on things, especially math. She couldn't sit still anymore, and her teacher reported a problem with her reading. "She reads perfectly to me," Maria said, "and her spelling is really good too. But she refused to read out loud, so the teacher never knew how she could read." This upset Maria, because it reminded her of Dorothea at that age.

Maria said Dorothea is 38 now, and she still can't read out loud. "The school would say it was her attitude," Maria said. "You know, it's so hard when you don't know what it is. Or in Danielle's case, you know and you cannot do anything about it."

Maria told me that her daughter and her granddaughter had many difficulties that were nearly identical: the inability to focus, lying, lack of interest in food (except candy), friendships only with boys, high energy, defiance, anger, manipulative behaviour, black-and-white thinking, inability to understand consequences, a disconnection between what they say and what they think, lack of boundaries, emotional immaturity. On the plus side, they both have big hearts, Maria said; they both love to work with children, and they want so much to be loved themselves.

For Maria, the biggest issue was lying. "They believe their own lies," Maria said. Dorothea and Maria have a good enough relationship now that they can talk about the lying, and Dorothea has told her she now knows when she's lying and Dorothea admits she believes her own lies. Maria told me Danielle's grade 7 teacher phoned her because she was concerned about Danielle's lies. Maria gave me some examples. Danielle said she had a horse and bragged to her classmates about her biological father, even though she'd never met him and didn't know who he was. She made up a story that her father wrote a science fiction book that became a popular TV series, and she knew how the series was going to end. Maria told me she's sure this story came up because Danielle was ashamed to admit she had no father and was living with her grandparents.

Maria said the lies are mostly about silly things. Both Danielle and Dorothea have made up stories about things that never happened. Miguel, she said, lived at home until the day he got married, and after he moved out, Dorothea lived with him for a while. Dorothea would say, "Mom, do you remember when I did things with Miguel?" Like he used to lock his bedroom door, and she'd use a key to come in, and he didn't like that. "But," Maria insisted, "he never had a lock on his bedroom!"

Maria said she learned the hard way not to confront them about their lies. She tried doing that with Dorothea, and that only made their relationship more difficult. She said it became part of the family culture that they would go along with stories Dorothea told, even though they knew they were untrue. Maria said now that Danielle is 16, Maria knows that spinning out imaginary stories as if they were true is part of who Danielle and Dorothea are.

Understanding consequences is another major problem. Curfews are important with all teenage girls, but how do you enforce them when the girl doesn't get the concept of consequences? "Your verbal skills have to be *so-o-o* good!" Maria explained. When Danielle broke curfew, Maria would sit down with her and explain that the next time she wouldn't be allowed to go out. "Oh my goodness!" Maria said. "They don't get it! They forget. They don't do it on purpose. So the next time you're gonna have the same problem. You have to deal with each day, right now. No tomorrows. They don't understand tomorrow."

"Promise" is a word Maria learned not to use, for the same reason. She says, "I will see" instead. If Danielle asks whether she can do something two days from now, "Don't ever say yes. You have to say 'We'll see.' " Maria said, "They fight you and fight you. It's always a fight with them. They cannot reason." The world is a slippery, mixed-up place for them, "and it's not their fault."

Now that Danielle has moved back in with her mother, they have a good relationship because they have so much in common. Maria said that growing up, they both complained to her whenever she told them to do more than one thing at a time, like take your plate to the kitchen and then go clean up your room. Dorothea has problems now getting Danielle to clean up her bedroom, Maria said, so Maria does it with her, hoping that by modeling good behaviour, eventually it might become a habit.

Maria and Dorothea have a good relationship now and talk on the telephone frequently. In fact, Maria said Dorothea tells her more than she needs to know. "Dorothea understands Danielle. She has the same disability. She's working with her and working with me. Every day Dorothea calls me and tells me what Danielle had for breakfast. Not that I have to know. And when she went to school and when she comes back and where she's going. Everything. She wants my advice. She wants to know she's doing the right thing for her daughter." But Dorothea drew the line at the FASD diagnosis. Danielle knows that she and her mom have similar disabilities, but Danielle didn't know her own disabilities were the result of her mother's drinking. Dorothea was afraid Danielle would find out.

When I met with her, Maria was in the middle of a struggle to get an FASD diagnosis for Danielle. She discovered at a grandparent support group meeting that having an official diagnosis could get Danielle a teacher's aide and access to a special program more suited to how she learned. She'd heard about a young man with FASD who got help, completed a university degree, and started a successful career as a teacher. Maria wanted Danielle to have the same opportunity.

Maria got Danielle's doctor to send documentation to the Glenrose Hospital in Edmonton to start the FASD assessment process. The Glenrose said they would take her in three months instead of placing her on the usual two-year waiting list, so Maria was happy about that. But in her application, Maria said Dorothea was willing to admit to drinking during pregnancy only if that admission was kept secret from Danielle. The FASD clinic told Maria they could have done that if Danielle were younger, but not when she's sixteen. They said they need to talk to Dorothea directly. Maria told them her daughter has FASD too, "so I have to deal with her." The person at the clinic said, "Okay, but try to get her to talk to me too."

"I called her the same way she manipulates Danielle," Maria laughed. "I'm a good manipulator. I threatened her. I told her the hospital called, but they need to talk to you and because Danielle's sixteen, she has to know. But she didn't want to. She said no, no, no. She wouldn't say anything." Maria gave Dorothea the number and told her she had to call. Dorothea said, "I don't want to because Danielle will find out. She's gonna hate me. We have a good relationship, and now you're gonna ruin everything!"

Maria said, "Manuel and I will tell her if you don't, and you'll have to tell her sometime anyway; she's gonna find out. Now is the time. If you don't, the hospital is gonna close the file and the assessment isn't gonna be done!" Finally, Dorothea relented and said she would call, and she did. But the clinic still needed paperwork from the school. An assessment the school did on Danielle was outdated and had to be redone. Maria and Manuel had legal guardianship of Danielle for fourteen years, but when Dorothea got married to a stable man and established a good home, Dorothea took Danielle back and became her legal guardian. So now Dorothea had to request the paper-work from the school; Maria didn't have the authority.

When I met with Maria, the request form had been in Dorothea's hands for two weeks. "I know she doesn't want to, because she doesn't want Danielle to know," Maria said. "So every day on the phone I ask her, 'Did you fill out the paper?' 'I'll do it today,' she says. 'I'll do it today!' And it hasn't been done."

Despite her difficulties with consequences, Dorothea understood all too well at this point in her life that her own drinking during pregnancy caused Danielle's dis-ability just as her own mother's drinking caused hers. The shame of it can be enough to overwhelm any young mother who is already struggling with addiction, self-esteem, and depression, and is probably not neurologically or emotionally mature.

A social worker told me of a disturbing case that drama-tized just how profound a mother's shame can be. He had plenty of experience talking with mothers of FASD chil-dren, and he always focused on the child's future when he discussed with the mother the importance of verifying that she drank during pregnancy. He would say, "Your child's future will be better if you sign this letter. She'll have access to a disability pension, get support in school, and her doctors will understand her better and be able to give her better care. Her foster parents will benefit too. You will be giving her a great gift by doing this." He said he thought he'd defused the blame issue with this mother. He was pleased about how he'd handled it and hopeful about the future for both mother and child. The mother signed the letter and convinced him that she understood this was about the future, not the past. But that same night, he said, the shame overwhelmed her, and she took her own life.

When I visited Betty Cornelius in McArthur Mills, Ontario, I told her this story. She was angry that this kind of thing is still happening. She said there's a clinic in downtown Toronto that does FASD diagnosis without insisting on what amounts to a confession from the mother. She said that the clinic, which is in St. Michael's Hospital, conducts the diagnostic work if there are reasonable grounds to suspect the mother drank during pregnancy. The word of a grandmother is sometimes enough. Other clinics across the country are moving in that direction, but many are not.

Like Maria, a great many grandparents don't know anything about FASD until it hits their grandchildren. When my own children were born, between 1977 and 1983, the science on FASD was in its infancy. It was on the fringes of even well-educated parents' awareness. The young parents I knew back then wondered what this worry about pregnancy and alcohol could mean, but most of us filed it away with the reports of competing scientific studies and expert opinions or stories on the daily news like: "seat belts save lives" and "seat belts cause serious abdominal injury" or "AIDS only a danger to gays" and "you can get AIDS from a toilet seat."

Back then most of us thought it didn't make sense that a woman's drinking during pregnancy could injure her baby; after all, look at how many previous generations of mothers drank and had healthy babies. What we ignored, though, was that most "respectable" women simply didn't drink in those days, and if they did, people denied it and didn't talk about it. It was culturally unacceptable. The liquor industry only started cultivating the female market in the 1980s and '90s, and since then women's liquor consumption has skyrocketed.[7] So has the rate of FASD. Meanwhile, skipped-generation grandparents have to deal every day with erratic behaviour and out-of-control emotions. When they face those difficulties, their own self-care is just as important as determining whether the cause is FASD, traumatic attachment disorder, or something else.

The next chapter presents a Saturday morning in the life of a set of grandparents struggling to balance self-care and their love for a grandchild who exhibits many of the signs of FASD.

---

7   For a complete analysis of the recent impact of alcohol on women, see Johnson, *Drink*.

TWELVE

In the Line of Fire:
Shell Shock and Self-Care

In the event of decompression, an oxygen mask
will automatically appear in front of you. Place it
firmly over your nose and mouth, secure the elastic
band behind your head, and breathe normally.
If you are travelling with a child, secure your
mask first, and then assist the other person.
                              —Flight attendant to passengers
                                         prior to takeoff

Last night, gramma was out late with a friend, and grampa was in charge. At eleven o'clock, he heard a thump in 8-year-old Nancy's bedroom. He dropped his book on the floor and ran upstairs. Nancy shrieked, "WAAA! WAAA! WAAAAAAAA!!!!" When he got to her bedroom, she was staring at the closet door, shaking, shivering. He put his arms around her, but she shouted even louder and pushed him away.

Her 10-year-old sister Amy stood in the hall, rubbing her eyes. "Why does she always do this?" she moaned, half asleep. Grampa went to her and said, "She's not awake. This isn't something she decides to do, you know. I'm sure this isn't fun for her either." He hugged Amy and asked her to go back to bed. While he did that, Nancy ran into the master bedroom and sat on gramma's side of the bed. She yelled, "Gramma! Gramma! I want GRAMMA!!!!"

Grampa stood next to her and hugged her again. She yelled into his ear, but he held her tight. She yelled even louder, "GRAMMA! GRAMMA! GRAMMA!" and pushed him away.

"If only gramma were here!" grampa thought. "She would work her magic and settle Nancy down, like she always does." He said to himself, "Nancy's just a little girl. I can handle her. I can do this." But his own kids never had night terrors. He's new at this. He wondered: What did somebody do to Nancy when she was little that makes her act like this? She yelled "GRAMMA! GRAMMA! GRAMMA!" no matter what he did. He remembered stories of parents duct-taping their kids' mouths shut to keep them quiet. "If this were the 1950s, when I was growing up," he thought, "I could lock her in her room and let her yell until she fell asleep." His arms felt stronger as he imagined strapping grey duct tape over her mouth and locking her in her room. But it's 2015! He decided to keep it simple: watch her to make sure she doesn't harm herself or anyone else, but let her sleepwalk and go wherever she will.

Nancy walked down the hall, still screaming, "Gramma! Gramma!" She went down the stairs, then into the bathroom. She shut the door. Slowly, her screams tapered off. Grampa waited outside the door. No whimpering or whining, no tinkling in the toilet, no flushing, no water running. Silence. When she opened the door, he took her hand and said, "Let's go back to bed." Her eyes were open, staring straight ahead, directly through him, as if he wasn't there. He tucked her back into bed. She rolled over and was suddenly still as a stone. He went to Amy's room, hugged her, kissed her on the cheek, and told her, "I wonder what's going on in her head, what makes her get up and scream like that." Amy's breathing is shallow, and her whole body shudders with every breath. Grampa wonders if Amy even heard him and whether she's awake or not. It's hard to tell, because when Amy doesn't want to talk, she pretends to be asleep.

The next morning, grampa lounges on his chesterfield in the living room, the front section of the *Edmonton Journal* open on his lap. He sips his coffee, sets it back on the side table, and turns the page. A cool westerly breeze tickles the hair on his bare legs. He opened the doors and windows when he got up at 6:00 and the sun was still low in the sky. July 9: the forecast says another dry, 30 degree day. It's 7:30 now. Everybody else in the house is asleep. A woodpecker tap-tap-taps on a poplar tree in the backyard.

Grampa's nose has run like a leaky faucet every day for the last three months. So many pollens and dust particles in the air! Every morning a blocked nostril or a sneeze wakes him up too early. But if he's slept five good hours without having to get up to pee, this quiet time is a gift: free respite, as refreshing as a sliver of retirement in Florida. If gramma could only worry less and sleep more, she could be up with him, enjoying their imaginary cottage on a beach together, just the two of them.

Since school let out two weeks ago, Nancy and Amy can sleep in. They need to. At this latitude the sun is up until 10:00 p.m. and daylight lingers until 11:00 this time of year, so they think they should be up late too. When they finally go to sleep, gramma and grampa have barely enough energy to watch an hour of television before they nod off. The last couple of years, they've gone out on dates once or twice a month. For people on pensions, though, babysitting is expensive: $10 an hour doubles or triples the cost of a night out. Then there's the hassle of trying to find a trustworthy teenager who lives close and has free time in his or her schedule between commitments to soccer, hockey, track and field, ballet, band, boyfriends, girlfriends, et cetera.

The most important babysitter qualifications, though, are assertiveness and creativity: get Nancy to bed by 8:30, supervise Amy, and referee when they fight. When Nancy teaches art to the sitter in her imaginary grade 2 classroom, the sitter has to keep her eye on the clock. She must allow an hour for the bedtime snack, which Nancy stretches into a four-course meal, lingering over each slice of peanut butter toast, each apple wedge, each plate of leftover rice, each cookie and dish of ice cream, and moaning after every course, "I'll die if I don't get more to eat! I'm starving!" or, "Don't we have a rule that kids can't go to bed hungry?" The babysitter has to cut Nancy off after the tuck-in when she begs, "Just one more story," or, "Just one more hug and I'll go to sleep. I promise!" And the babysitter has to be mature enough to stay calm if Nancy has a night terror.

On this cool summer morning, grampa knows Nancy might come down the stairs at any time. He's glad for every quiet minute and every sip of hot coffee. As he reads about ISIS beheadings in Syria, random shootings in California, the latest book and movie reviews, Nancy's latest night terror fades from his mind.

At 7:45 Nancy thumps down the stairs. Grampa says, "Good morning, Nancy!" and extends his arms for a hug. She walks past him, picks up the TV remote from the coffee table, turns to him, flutters her eyelashes, and says in a syrupy-sweet voice, "Can I watch TV? I promise I'll keep the sound down real low."

"No, Nancy," he says. "We don't want you watching TV in the morning."

"You *never* let me watch TV!" she shrieks. The same shriek as last night. Grampa sets the newspaper down on the floor. He thinks, "How can I keep her from waking up gramma and Amy?" "What if I can't handle her today? What if gramma hasn't slept enough?" He remembers his first run at parenthood, how his ex-wife always seemed better at settling kids down than he was.

Nancy aims the remote at the television, her right index finger on the Power button. "I'm going to watch it anyway," she says, her eyes twinkling like a princess who knows she'll get her way. Then the twinkle turns to ice. "And you can't stop me!" Grampa's heart races. The same way it did during his marriage breakup when he told his ex how he felt and she kept shouting. The same as when the ex used to switch from yelling rage to seductive, sexy sweetness when she wanted something from him.

Grampa takes a deep breath, counts to ten in his head, smiles, and says, "What would you like for breakfast, Nancy?" He hopes changing the subject will do the trick. After all, she's good at distracting herself.

Nancy lowers the remote and lies flat on the chesterfield, face down, her arms spread wide. She kicks the cushions, right left, right left, right left, like a kick-boxer pummeling an opponent she's knocked to the canvas. "I wanna watch TV!" she yells.

"How about a boiled egg?" he says. "Or Cocoa Mini-Wheats? Cinnamon Toast Crunch?"

"I don't know what I wanna eat!" she shrieks. "I wanna watch TV!"

Grampa gets up from his chair and walks over to Nancy, sits next to her, and reaches down to hug her. She's rigid as a log and pushes him away. "Why don't you get dressed for the day," he says, "and then I can feed you."

"No!" she yells. "I don't want to." She kicks the chesterfield some more.

He decides to let her be, give her time. He goes into the kitchen, cracks two eggs into a skillet, pops a slice of bread into the toaster, and pours himself a second cup of coffee.

"Why do you get to use your iPhone and your computer all the time?" she yells. "And you won't let us even watch TV! *It's not fair!!!!*"

"I use those things for work," he says.

She sits up and aims the remote at the TV again.

"I said no TV!" he says, louder than the last time.

"I hate you!" she yells. "I *hate* you! I want gramma!"

"Gramma's still sleeping," he says. "Leave her alone. Go get dressed, and you can have some breakfast."

Nancy lies face down on the chesterfield again. She plays dead.

Grampa flips his scrambled eggs onto a plate, spreads apricot jam on his toast, and takes his breakfast and coffee over to the dining room table. He reads the *Avenue* magazine that came with the morning paper. Nancy walks over and stands next to him. He finishes his eggs and half his toast and turns the page. She sees an ad for women's high-heeled shoes. It's a full-page, full-colour ad featuring a slender, long-legged woman in a bright pink evening gown, low-cut at the neck to reveal the sides of both breasts. The fabric and her skin both glisten like satin.

"I want that ad!" she shouts in his ear.

"Keep your voice down," grampa says. He wants to shout back, to match her decibel for decibel, but he remembers that he's the adult in the room. "People are sleeping."

"But I want that ad!" she shouts again.

"No!" he says firmly, proud that he's able to keep his voice down, despite the temptation to raise it. His heart races faster. His gut is tangled tight like a fishing line backlash. "I'm reading. You can't have the ad."

She lowers her voice, imitating a prissy teenage girl she's watched on a TV sitcom. "I'll get dressed," she says breathily, smirking like she's already won. "*If* you give me the ad." Grampa laughs at the absurdity: here's an 8-year-old girl playing Marilyn Monroe, the femme fatale who could make all the penises in a room stand at attention and march the barely functioning male brains they're connected to over a cliff. He strangles the laugh before it reaches his mouth.

"No deal!" he says. He's met pseudo-Marilyns before. He got sucked in when he was 16. He detests them and the puddle of hormones they reduced him to. The anger and disgust rush into his face and voice. He pinches his lips. His words chase each other at a gallop. The pitch of his voice jumps from bass to tenor. "You have to get dressed! And you have to eat before you go anywhere!"

"Well!" she huffs, her lips tightly pursed, her arms folded close to her chest. She reads emotions better than she reads words. She knows she's as good as won. "I just won't then! I want that ad!"

Grampa turns back to his food. He's been through too many yes-you-will, no-I-won't confrontations with kids. He knows that won't work. He over-chews the last bite of toast and washes it down with a gulp of coffee. He thinks, "How can I get through to this kid? Threaten to cut her off TV for a week? She lives only in the present. She doesn't know what day of the week it is or how long a week is.

She'll forget this as quickly as she did last night's terror. She needs to have control, because when she was little, her mother was often too high to change her diaper, no matter how long she cried. But she can't win this time!"

He knows what won't work, but he doesn't know what will. He knows Nancy is determined to win. His egg, toast, jam, and coffee all sit at the top of his clenched stomach. A wave of nausea surges over him. His breakfast could as easily come back up as go down. "Maybe giving her the ad is a good compromise?" he thinks. "It's just an *f*-ing ad I don't want! Maybe then she won't think about the TV anymore. It'll be a win-win situation."

He rips the page out, throws it at her, and says, "Here!" He's still mad about the pseudo-Marilyns he fell for when he was a kid. He's mad that he has to spend so much energy battling kids instead of doing grownup things with 60-year-old friends. He can't even play cards at the senior centre because after he subtracts kid time from his week—including the time it takes to cool off after these confrontations—the week is over. Did he even win the TV battle for today? The nausea tells him he's lost all around.

He gets up from the table and drops his plate, cutlery, and coffee cup into the sink. He stands next to Nancy, bends down, and looks her in the eye. His voice is thin and strained from trying to keep the anger out of it. He says, "I've had enough of you this morning." He takes a deep breath. "I love you, but you cannot order me around and defy me like this. Stay away from me."

He goes upstairs to the master bedroom, where gramma is just getting dressed. It's 8:30. "You take her," he says through gritted teeth. "She's been rude and nasty to me all morning. I've had enough! I need a time out!" Gramma nods. They both struggle with Nancy, and sometimes gramma has to break away too.

Grampa gets clean underwear out of his dresser, steps into the bathroom, and closes the door. He takes the shower he decided not to take earlier because it could have awakened gramma and Amy. He brushes his teeth and shaves. The routine is comforting, but his body is still clenched in anger. He dresses himself, stashes a novel and a writing pad in his backpack, walks downstairs, and passes through the kitchen on his way out of the house. Gramma, Nancy, and Amy are eating breakfast. They look up. Nancy walks over to him and whimpers, "I'm sorry, Grampa."

Grampa knows this is a positive sign, but he's heard "sorry" so many times before, and the defiance keeps coming back. Nancy must think the word works like the magic silver pen Will Smith uses on people in *Men in Black* to erase the memory of the aliens they just saw. Maybe that's just how Nancy's mind works when she asks every morning, "Is today a school day?"

He says to himself, "She probably doesn't even remember what she did. She only knows I'm upset and it has something to do with her. I'll forgive her, but how can I help her do better the next time?"

He takes a deep breath, bends down, and looks her in the eye. "Sorry just isn't good enough, Nancy. You keep doing this kind of thing again and again. If you really are sorry, you have to prove it to me. You have to do better next time. You have to do what we tell you to do. We are in charge here. Not you."

He gives her a hug, kisses gramma and Amy, and walks out the front door. After several hours walking in the park along the river, reading, journaling, he's still full from breakfast. His scrambled eggs still sit in that same spot on top of his clenched stomach, ready to come up or go down. His lower back muscles are tight and sore. His head is throbbing. His heart is a fist, his entire gut a tangled knot. He wonders, "Why am I trying to raise two damaged kids? I'm sixty-six years old. How long before I get to retire like a normal person and do something I really want to do?"

When he talks to gramma later that afternoon, she says Nancy cried when he left and asked her, "Is grampa ever coming back?" Nancy was sure she was being abandoned again and that it's been her fault both times.

An image from three years before flashes before him. The Saturday morning he told Nancy he was moving the car out of the driveway and parking it on the street in front of the house. He started the car. She immediately ran to the driver's window, screaming. She banged her fists on the glass to stop him. In his mind, she's banging the glass again, her wailing mouth open wide. Tears well up in his eyes. The nausea lingers, strong as ever. Even after a day alone to walk it off and think it out, his body won't let it go. But at least he didn't make things worse at home. He took a day-long time out and took care of himself.

When he imagines the future, he wonders if Nancy will learn to regulate herself better before she's a teenager, when she's going through puberty, and her hormones are out of control, and she'll be using makeup and wearing dresses that would have been too short even for Marilyn Monroe. When he's feeling especially hopeful, he even imagines Nancy and Amy someday thanking him and gramma for everything they've done to make a better life for them.

If he met Betty Cornelius, he'd be even more hopeful. Despite being abandoned by her mother at the age of three and her certainty that she has FASD herself, sixty years from now Nancy could be the next Betty: a community leader and a role model for grandparents.

THIRTEEN

I Survive, I Rescue, I Organize: The Roaring Grandma

I'm in the rescue business: dogs, cats, and kids.
—*Betty Cornelius, founder of* CANGRANDS

B etty Cornelius is living proof that someone whose mother drank heavily during pregnancy can live a long and productive life. She's 63, and she talks like she's just getting started. Betty was quiet as a mouse most of her life, after a childhood of abandonment, abuse, and put-downs, but she's been a roaring grandmother bear since 1980.

Betty's goal is a Canada-wide organization of 75,000 grandparent-caregivers with the political clout in every province and territory to get laws passed and funds appropriated so that grandparents don't have to give up their life savings, their homes, and their retirements to raise grandchildren. The way we treat these grandparents, she says, is a form of elder abuse. Too many won't speak up for themselves—because of shame, fear of losing custody of or contact with grandchildren, and fear of alienating their own children—so Betty is leading the charge against what she calls "gagged grandparents syndrome."

I discovered Betty Cornelius and CANGRANDS in 2012, less than two years after I became a skipped-generation grandfather. I phoned her, and since then I've received between five and fifteen emails or Facebook posts a day from CANGRANDS, most from Betty herself. I met Betty at the CANGRANDS summer camp that year in Ameliasburgh, Ontario.

In October 2015, Betty invited me to spend two days with her and her husband at their home in McArthur's Mills, Ontario, a forty-five-minute drive from Bancroft, the nearest town. To get to Bancroft from Toronto's West End took me over three hours, the last half of it on a narrow highway more crooked than a bent-up corkscrew. It was unsafe to go over eighty kilometres an hour and unsafe to pull off and gape at the scenery: the grey granite hills, the Group of Seven–style pine trees, bent and lonely and jutting out of the rocks, the orange and red and yellow maples lit up like jagged little suns whenever the low-hanging clouds briefly parted. People come from far away every fall to see this magnificent display, but I was on a mission and couldn't stop.

When I pulled up in the driveway of 2580 Hartsmere Road, Weslemkoon Lake was right in front of me, a vast mirror of shimmering sunshine, blue sky, and fall colour. Betty and her pet chihuahua welcomed me. Betty said

Bella was a rescue dog who had been overbred, and that she used to lie on her back and pee on herself whenever a man came near. I was glad to hear she was over that. But Bella had a chronic lung condition. At least once every hour her little chest would heave and clench, and she'd cough over and over as if she'd inhaled a chicken bone.[1]

Betty told me she's rescued other dogs and cats too, as well as thirty-two foster children, a neighbour's grandson, and her own 22-year-old granddaughter, Crystal. When Betty told me her own life story, I realized she's rescued at least one other person: herself. Betty's life may have been even rougher than Bella's.

Betty was the child of an alcoholic, abusive mother. She simply left Betty in the hospital for six weeks after she was born; she didn't want her. Betty's grandmother raised her for six years but became too ill to keep her, and so she returned Betty to her mother. Betty's stepfather raped her repeatedly, she told me, and so did some of her mother's other boyfriends. Her mother called her "a worthless little slut." Betty jumped from a three-story building at age 8, the first of three suicide attempts before she was 21. Her mother beat her often. She threw Betty down the stairs when Betty was pregnant at 16, saying, "I hope your baby dies!" Later, Betty learned from her grandmother that, as a child, Betty's mother was loaned to a neighbour for sex in return for food so the family could eat.

---

1 About six weeks after my visit, Betty was mourning Bella's death.

Betty took on the "worthless little slut" label and lived the part. "I used to say, 'I'm dressing the twins up and going out for the night' and shake my boobies," she told me. "I was gonna get laid!" When she wasn't acting out sexually, Betty learned to be quiet and keep her head down. Because of the abuse, she couldn't even look people in the eye. She was a mouse back then, she said.

She gave birth to two sons, one an Rh-negative baby who's been blind, deaf, and totally handicapped his whole life, and who now lives in an institution in Edmonton. The other is a 40-year-old, welfare-dependent addict who was kicked out of school, had numerous run-ins with police, beat Betty up for money, and fathered Betty's grand-daughter, Crystal. His last message to Betty was a Mother's Day greeting: "Go Fuck Yourself!" To top it off, Betty spent $28,000 on lawyers to get custody of Crystal from her parents and to protect Crystal from her abusive mater-nal grandparents. Clearly, Betty knows from experience that not all grandparents are good for their grandchildren.

When her sons were little—one of them on oxygen—Betty hitchhiked from Vermilion to Edmonton to escape from an abusive husband. She cared for her sons in her home as a single mother while she put herself through college, despite a car accident that put her in a neck brace and temporarily immobilized one arm. Listening to her story, I remembered the hard-luck Joe Btfsplk in the *Li'l Abner* cartoon strip from when I was a boy. He always had a storm cloud lingering over his head; if something could go wrong for him, it did.

The birth of Betty's first child turned her mother around. She said her mother was "a horrible mom" but "a terrific gramma." "We had eleven years of healing," Betty told me. Then, in 1980, Betty's life took another turn when an ex-boyfriend murdered Betty's mother. Four days later, her mother's then boyfriend set her house on fire with people in it. And he molested Betty the day of the funeral!

"I'm bent over the dishwasher," she said, "and he bent over me and grabbed my boobs and said, 'I miss your mom so much!' I took a knife out of the dishwasher and backed him up into a corner of the house. I said, 'I will hurt you! I will stab you!' I just went insane. How I didn't stab him is a miracle. But that's the last time anybody ever abused me. Nobody is ever going to do that again! Lord help them!" Suddenly, she became Betty the Bear.

The Bear has been on a tear ever since, fighting for dogs, cats, kids, and grandparents. Her own granddaughter, Crystal, was born with a triple heart condition, a stomach hernia, a collapsed lung, serious FASD, and during child-hood was poisoned four times, thrown across the room, and suffered other, worse abuse Betty didn't want to talk about. When Betty told me all the battles she fought for Crystal, it was clear to me that she protected and fought for Crystal as aggressively as any black or grizzly bear. Get between a mother bear and her cub, and she will rip you apart to protect her young. That's Betty. And she's determined not to let four, seven, or maybe even more generations of abuse and FASD slow her down.

Betty told me she's sure sexual abuse in her family goes back at least three generations, and that alcohol abuse may go even further. Like most of her generation, she grew up not knowing about FASD. Diagnostic procedures for FASD did not exist, and nobody knew much about it, but Betty is sure she has it. She's got papers to prove Crystal has it too. Crystal has a lifelong disability pension because of prenatal, alcohol-caused brain damage. All through school, Betty told me, she taught Crystal's teachers how to teach her. She tutored Crystal herself for two hours every summer morning, and Crystal now has a high school diploma and a year of college behind her.

FASD manifests itself in many different ways. Betty described what it's done to Crystal. "She doesn't understand touch," Betty told me. "I'd walk in and touch her shoulder, and she'd say, 'What did you hurt me for?' I'd say, 'I didn't hurt you.' 'Yes you did!' 'I just touched you! Crystal, if I did that'"—Betty whacked a book against the coffee table so hard the floor shook—"that would be hurting you." Even then, Crystal would insist, "No! You hurt me, Grandma!"

Crystal had a hard time reading facial features and tones of voice too. "I'd say to her in a normal tone of voice, 'Crystal, can you pick that up?' And she'd say, 'Why are you nagging me? Why are you yelling at me?' *That's* fetal alcohol."

Betty gave me a demonstration. "I said to her"—Betty switched to her deepest and angriest mother bear voice— "THIS IS HOW I SOUND WHEN I'M MAD!" She switched back to her normal, pleasant Betty voice and said, "This is how I normally talk." She switched back to the angry voice, "AND NOW I'M NOT HAPPY!" She used an even louder, angrier voice to say, "*AND NOW I'M REALLY NOT HAPPY!*" And she'd say, "Crystal, can you hear the difference?" Then Betty smiled and said, "Crystal, look at my face. This is my happy face." Betty pinched her face tight around her mouth and scowled. "*This is when I'm not very happy with you, Crystal!*" Betty said she repeated the lesson often, and whenever Crystal read her the wrong way, Betty corrected her with another demonstration and asked, "Does this look like my happy face?"

Betty got even more creative about teaching Crystal money management, which Crystal still hasn't mastered. The lessons started with tithing in church. When Crystal got an allowance or a monetary gift, Betty divided it up: 20 per cent for Crystal's long-term savings bank, 10 per cent for her short-term savings bank, and 10 per cent for her blessing bank. The other 60 per cent Crystal could spend on candy, junk, whatever she wanted. Betty promised not to criticize or comment on how she spent that 60 per cent. Crystal often broke things, like a portable DVD player, so Betty looked up the cost, and Crystal would either have to replace them herself or do without. That's what the short-term savings were for.

On a trip to Sick Kids Hospital in Toronto, Crystal started working out the rules for the blessing bank. They walked past some homeless people, and afterwards Crystal asked, "Do I *have* to give it to the church?" She said she wanted to buy socks and snacks to help the homeless. Betty agreed that was a good way to use the money. In fact, Betty was so impressed, she bragged about Crystal online, and somebody sent Crystal $100, and another one $20, for her "socks and sustenance fund."

Teaching the Ontario government about money has been an even bigger battle for Betty, and she's still fighting it. She told me that Crystal gets a disability cheque for over a thousand dollars every month because of FASD. When Crystal turned 18, she got two major credit cards. Because she reached that magic number, Ontario Works decided Crystal should get the disability cheque directly instead of having it go to Betty. Betty told the worker, "Are you crazy? If you allow her to manage her money by herself, she's going to end up on the street because she's not gonna pay her rent, she's gonna max out her credit cards, and drop out of college!" Three years later, Betty's predictions all came true. Crystal had her phone cut off too, and collection agencies were coming after her.

So Betty phoned the worker again and "just laid into her. The worker says, 'I can't talk to you.' Well, you can friggin' well listen!" Betty said. She told the worker what had happened and added, "I might end up with a great-grandbaby to raise, and if that happens, I'm dropping her off on your doorstep, *'cause I'm not doing any of that!*" Since then, Betty has managed to convince at least one worker to keep sending cheques to the grandparents, but she told me that if an adult with FASD wants to receive his own cheques, he can—even though the brain damage he's getting the disability payment for is the reason he doesn't know how to manage the money!

But it's not enough for Betty to advocate only for herself and Crystal. She told me that she realized twenty years ago that she'd get farther with politicians and government officials if she represented a group, not just herself. In 1997, the issue was Crystal's parents denying Betty access to Crystal when they broke up. She organized some local grandparents in the Toronto area and got Bill 27 through the Ontario Legislature to help ensure that in most cases grandparents can get access to their grandchildren.

When Betty moved to the Bancroft area, she created a provincial grandparents group through the internet, which evolved into a Facebook group with 280 members across the country. When I spoke with her, Betty had over 700 more on her personal contact list. People post links to articles they find about grandparenting, FASD, drug addiction, court battles, schooling, illnesses, as well as anything they want to say about what's bothering them, what they've been doing, battles won or lost with doctors, teachers, lawyers, judges, social workers. There's never a shortage of issues, but finding the time and the freedom to do something about those issues is difficult, even for grandparents who don't have to go out and earn a living.

Betty somehow finds the energy to organize and fight even though she works part-time. Recently, her battles with the Ontario government have been about money. Grandparents in Ontario get $250 a month per child—if they get anything at all—but for the same child, a foster parent would get $900 to $1,500 a month. "This is what they deem to be the cost of raising that child in your home," Betty said. "It's expenses! It's not income!" That's why it's not taxable. So why would two branches of the same Ontario government say this child costs $250 to raise in a kinship home and $1,500 to raise in a foster home? Betty says this is discrimination against the grandchild and a form of elder abuse.

Betty told me there are forty-six Children's Aid Society (CAS) offices in Ontario and twenty-seven Ontario Works offices, and that each office has its own guidelines. Ontario Works administers the temporary care allowance (TCA). Betty said that when she got her first Ontario Works cheque, it was called "foster care money," but then they changed it to the TCA in 2008. With the name change, Betty says, "they started cutting people off in Hamilton, Ottawa, one by one," because they had the children full-time, not temporarily. Betty got a call from a grandmother in Oshawa who said she didn't get her November cheque, that she phoned and Ontario Works told her she was cut off. "She started bawling. She said, 'I need that cheque to feed my grandson and to help with Christmas. I can't have Christmas now!'" Betty heard from others too, and people started phoning government offices, MPPs, and the media. She said Madeleine Meilleur, the minister of community and social services, went on national television and told grandparents that if they couldn't afford to keep their grandchildren, to turn them in to the government. Betty called on grandparents to bring dolls representing their grandchildren and to make a spectacle of the minister's callous attitude. Betty said 200 grandparents handed in 900 dolls. They didn't get the policy reversed, but thanks to Pro Bono Law Ontario and others, individual grandparents appealed, 98 per cent of whom had their funding reinstated.

But some grandparents simply would not appeal: this was just one more obstacle to climb, and they'd had enough. They'd rather suck it up, stretch their resources even further, lower their standard of living another notch, or delay retirement even longer. They were afraid the government would take their grandkids away if they complained. If not for Betty and CANGRANDS, none of them would have had much of a choice. Hundreds of grandparents would be isolated and ignorant of programs they qualify for, and unable to learn from other grandparents' experience.

Betty laughed when she thought about the fact that she runs a national organization from her bedroom in a house so far away from major population centres. She lives in almost total isolation, yet she got TVOntario to do a documentary on grandparenting; CTV's W5 did another one, and 100 Huntley Street did a couple of smaller ones. CANGRANDS, she said, has been in a hundred newspapers and on over a hundred radio programs.

Betty compared CANGRANDS to the Canadian National Institute for the Blind. The CNIB, she said, gets 29 per cent of its funding from various levels of government, and it supports 22,000 blind people in Ontario. "They have really lovely, high-gloss flyers and handouts," Betty said. "They have a 1-800 number with twenty-four-hour staff," and they provide technology, education, employment assistance, and other programs. For the same number of skipped-generation grandparents in Ontario, there's a tangle of irregular programs and financial support, and the only relevant organization for them is CANGRANDS, which Betty runs out of her bedroom, a forty-five-minute drive from Bancroft! In fact, 22,000 is the number of skipped-generation grandparents in Ontario that Statistics Canada officially recognizes, but Betty is certain the real number is much higher, since many grandparents are too ashamed or afraid even to seek help.

CANGRANDS gets no government funding and has no glossy brochures. It has a website (cangrands.com) and a business card with Betty's phone number and address. CANGRANDS has no budget beyond the $25 annual membership dues, which only a fraction of the members manage to pay. CANGRANDS has twenty-five to thirty chapters across the country and chapter leaders who organize meetings and support grandparents in their areas, but most of the leaders' energy goes into raising their own grandchildren.

CANGRANDS publicity? That's Betty herself, scattering business cards wherever she goes, like Johnny Appleseed. She walks into schools, talks to the secretaries, and leaves cards. On her travels, she leaves cards in washrooms and under napkin holders in restaurants. Betty told me about a call she just got from a grandmother who said, "I was in a Tim Hortons bathroom. I picked up this card and looked at it. I put it in my purse. That was three years ago. I don't know why I kept it." Then the grandmother cried. Her grandchild had just been apprehended, and she didn't know what to do. "That's exactly why I do it," Betty said.

She certainly doesn't do it because she wants people to recognize her as a hero, or even to thank her for what she does.

All the other skipped-generation grandparents I've met are also too busy parenting to worry about getting thanked and too focused on the daily challenges to think about the impact of their work on society, much less to imagine themselves as heroes. But while doing some totally unrelated work, I met a woman seventeen years younger than me who was proud to tell me about her personal hero, the woman who took her in at age 13 and was her entire family for the next thirty years: her grandmother.

FOURTEEN

Thank You, Grandma

To me, that's what love is all about: the sacrifices....
I don't know what I would've done without her.
—Karen, whose grandmother
took her in 40 years ago

In 1978, when she was 13, Karen ran away from home to live with her grandmother. Her stepfather terrified her. He was 33 years old, weighed 275 pounds, and had a build like a grizzly bear, with gargantuan hands to match. She weighed 115. If it ever came to a fight, Karen knew she wouldn't stand a chance. He always loomed over her as a threat, even when he wasn't nearby. Fear of him was her constant companion.

Thirty-four years later, Karen still had vivid memories of the purple welts he'd raised on her backside when he spanked her with his belt. Even worse, though, was an image seared into her brain as if with a glowing, red-hot cattle-branding iron. In the family kitchen, as Karen and her younger twin siblings looked on, her stepfather clenched those burly, thick fingers around her mother's throat and lifted her up off the floor. Her feet kicked and twitched in the air like a person with a rope around her neck hanging from a tree branch after a lynching.

Thirty-four years later, Karen's ears still rang with her stepfather's deep-throated rage, his cussing and name-calling as he held her mother in the air by her neck. That was the same voice he often used to criticize and command Karen and everyone else in the family. When she told me the story, she said she knew, beyond any doubt, that he'd assaulted her mother other times too, even though he and her mother did their best to hide it.[1] That time in the kitchen, she said, was the worst she ever saw.

I met Karen in September 2012 near Olds, Alberta, where we attended the annual national meeting of the Alternatives to Violence Project. We sat on the veranda of a dorm at the Church of the Nazarene Bible Camp, and she told me about her life with grandma. It was early evening, and the sun, nearly down to the horizon, backlit the spruce trees towering above us. Yellow trembling aspen leaves on the slope below glowed like sunflower petals and fluttered with every breath of wind. During our conversation, we often looked west toward the valley where a creek trickled between mud banks, cracked and dry from a summer of heat and drought.

---

1   I asked Karen if her stepfather's behaviour might have been caused by drugs or alcohol, as domestic violence often is. She told me he hardly drank at all and never used drugs.

That April weekend when Karen ran away from her parents, her family was camped out in their trailer in Ontario's cottage country, three and a half hours' drive from home. She told me her stepfather yelled at her yet again for being defiant, for not doing what he told her to do. She hated him and was afraid to be around him. She knew she couldn't win the battle, so she hid in a corner of the trailer.

"I refused to speak," she said. "I refused to eat. I just didn't want to interact with anybody. I was very angry. I was afraid that if I said anything, everything would explode." When the time came to pack up and leave, her stepfather barked out orders like a commandant, she said, and she obeyed because she knew that was the only way she could ever get home.

When they got home and began to unpack, he ordered her around some more: "Get this." "Move that." "Do this." Karen told me she felt like some sort of slave. "It was the tone of voice and the level of disrespect that I had such a hard time with," she said.

Just inside the main door to their bungalow was "a tiny landing," Karen said. The basement stairs ran straight down; the kitchen was on the left. Karen carried a load of food and cooking utensils from the trailer and pushed the door open, not gently but not violently either, she explained. She didn't know her mother—a rather petite woman—was on the other side. When the door handle rammed her in the side, Karen's mother yelled. Immediately, the stepfather pounced. He towered over

Karen and spewed out yet another stream of angry cuss-words and demanded she apologize to her mother.

"At that point, I'm not liking my mom very much," Karen said. "I would not have intentionally hurt her, but I'm very angry with my mom because she knows how this man has treated us." So Karen refuses to apologize.

"So my mom, right away says, 'No. She doesn't have to apologize.'" Karen's mom had years of experience trying to smooth things over and pacify her husband. It worked. He dropped the demand, but Karen was grounded for the night. She had to stay in her bedroom in the basement.

"I remember crying," Karen said. "I remember calling my grandmother, as I did so often when things went horribly wrong in the house." She and her grandmother agreed that Karen should walk to her grandmother's place the next day, Monday. Her house was twenty minutes away from the school and Karen would come during her lunch break. She was in grade 8. That night Karen didn't change into her pajamas because she was afraid her step-father would come down and hurt her, and she wanted to be ready to run if he did.

The next morning, Karen waited until everyone else left the house. She packed her duffle bag and a bag lunch and went to school. At lunch she and her grandmother agreed Karen would come back to grandma's house after school. Karen made grandma promise she wouldn't tell her mom where Karen was. Karen's mother was grandma's only child. Looking back on that day, Karen realized that was an impossible promise for her grandmother to keep. But when grandma phoned her mom at six o'clock, Karen was livid.

Almost immediately, her grandmother's sister and brother-in-law came to pick Karen up, and soon she was in the chief of police's office, answering questions. Then CAS got involved. Karen lived with her great-aunt and great-uncle and a cousin for two months, in a different part of the city. At that point, her grandmother agreed Karen could live with her. Her aunt and uncle would have taken her in, Karen said, but their house was too small.

One benefit of living with grandma, Karen said, was that when she started high school a couple of months later, she could go to the same school as her friends. The downside was that grandma's place was small, a one-bedroom apartment. Grandma gave Karen the bedroom, and for three years, grandma pulled out the sofa bed every night and slept there. Then grandma got a two-bedroom place across the hall; it wasn't much bigger, but the second bedroom meant a lot less work for grandma, and they both had more privacy.

Grandma lived alone and had no car. Her husband had died in 1968, the same year as Karen's father. Grandma was 69 when Karen moved in. Luckily, the grocery store was nearby, but shopping for food for herself and a teenager was a big job. Sometimes Karen helped, but mostly grandma took her cart to the bus stop, got on the bus, walked to the store, and on the return trip lugged 3-litre milk jugs and other heavy things up the stairs. She lived on a pension. She got minimal support from CAS for a while, Karen told me, and so grandma always did whatever she could to save money.

Karen said grandma was never very affectionate towards her, "but I knew she loved me. She would show her affection in the things she did. She would make me breakfast every morning. She would make me lunch."

That's the kind of person grandma was, Karen said. She always looked for ways to serve others. She volunteered at her church and at a nursing home, where she did sewing for people. Karen said that for months grandma helped a neighbour in her building who needed eye drops at certain times of the day and couldn't do it herself.

Karen told me that during the ten years she lived with grandma, she was not a difficult child and was very co-operative. She had no responsibilities except what she took on voluntarily. That included doing laundry and housework. "One of the things we joked about was, if it was raining, she'd say to me, 'Oh, dear! It's raining! You'd better stay home. I don't want you to sit in wet clothes. You just wait until the rain lets up.' I would just say, 'Thank you, Grandma.' When I told my friends at school, they'd laugh." Those rain delays were usually only half an hour or so, she said, but they were memorable times Karen and grandma had together. "When I was late for school," Karen said, "I'd write my own note and say, 'Grandma, would you sign this?' and she would." Grandma wasn't interested in having anything to do with the school, partly because she wasn't educated herself.

Karen's high school marks were mostly As, which surprised Karen herself, since she was used to getting Cs and Ds when she still lived with her mom and stepfather. In her first term, she got five As. "I remember being in math class and the teacher asked how many people got how many As." He started at one, and when he got up to five, Karen raised her hand. He asked her, "What did your parents think?" When Karen told him they didn't know, he was shocked. He didn't know she lived with grandma, and she hadn't volunteered the information.

Grandma never imposed a curfew on Karen, and Karen said she rarely abused the privilege. But one of the exceptions later became a highlight of her years with grandma, something they often joked about. Karen told me she was dating the high school boyfriend she would later marry. Sometimes she came home very late. One time he brought her home at 6:00 a.m. The doorknob and deadbolt were both locked. Karen had a key, but she worried about the noise she'd make unlocking them.

She got inside without a sound and crept slowly, quietly down the hall. She had to cross grandma's doorway to get to her own room. "As I pass her doorway," she said, "I let out a sigh of relief because I think I've done it. All of a sudden I hear her say, 'Why don't you just invite him in for breakfast?' "

Even after that, grandma didn't impose a curfew, but Karen said she felt "a bit of an edge" around her date nights, and so she never did anything like that again. Grandma never said anything else about it, but Karen understood grandma's concern for her safety and realized grandma worried when she didn't know where Karen was at night. As Karen's relationship with her boyfriend developed, grandma started looking out for him too. If it was snowing, she'd invite him to spend the night on the sofa bed instead of driving home, since he lived out of town.

Karen told me that grandma never did get legal custody of her. A CAS worker visited her mother and stepfather after Karen left, and that didn't go well. Her stepfather was uncooperative, angry that his mother-in-law had taken Karen in. But after a while, "there was never any discussion of me leaving grandma's place. Never brought up by CAS, my mother, or stepfather." Karen and her grandma got along well for the ten years they lived together. Then Karen moved out to get married. After her marriage broke up, she got a place one floor below grandma's and lived there a year and a half.

Karen told me she struggled to re-establish relationships with the rest of her family, but she never got very far. The first few times she visited her mother, they met at a neutral location, not at the family home. They continued to have contact every few months, but never got very close. Even so, Karen's mother gave her the financial support she needed to go to university, which Karen said was a big sacrifice for her. Karen said she never had good relationships with her stepfather or her younger brother and sister, who were twins, six years younger than Karen. Her sister left home at 14, Karen said, and her brother at 17 because it was such a stressful place. Her brother suffered from severe depression, spent time in a facility for troubled youth, and died in a car accident at the age of 21. Karen said that since her mother was an only child, she had no cousins, and so grandma, along with grandma's three sisters and one brother-in-law, were the only family she had.

When she'd been married two years, Karen realized her sister was struggling to finish high school, and so she took her in. That only lasted four months, and she and Karen have been distant from each other ever since.

It was different with grandma, though. Karen moved away from the city where grandma lived, but most of the time she was only about thirty kilometres away. Their relationship was strong for the next twenty years, until grandma died in 2008 at the age of 99. Often, grandma would come to stay with her for several days at a time. Towards the end of grandma's life, Karen insisted grandma stay with her when she was ill, so Karen could look after her. When grandma was in the hospital after a near-fatal heart attack, Karen spent a night curled up next to her on the bed.

Karen said that when grandma died, she was ready to let her go. By that time Karen had come to believe "that we are eternal beings, that we truly never die." So I asked her what she would say to grandma right now. "I often have little conversations with her," she said. "Many times I say thank you, thank you, thank you. Thank you for all the sacrifices you made. Because she did." Tears well up in Karen's eyes, and her voice breaks. She reaches in her pocket for a Kleenex to daub away the tears. "Because she did. She made many. To me, that's what love is all about, the sacrifices....I don't know what I would've done without her."

Karen told me she's worked at having a relationship with her stepfather, and has visited him and her mother together, but he hasn't changed. She said she "would have become a very angry, very bitter person" if she'd stayed with her parents. "I have never, ever had any regrets," she said, about leaving home.

Before I turned off the recorder, I asked Karen if she had anything to add. She immediately started weeping. When she gathered herself together and wiped away the tears, she said, "It's a wonderful thing just to know that somebody really cares, that somebody takes an interest in you." Then her voice broke so she couldn't speak at all. She turned away and wept again. Her chest heaved again and again as she sobbed. "Makes you feel wanted and special," she whimpered and wept again.

I wonder how many children could say something similar about child welfare caseworkers. There must be some, but I haven't met any. Most of the grandparents I've met who raise grandchildren roll their eyes and shrug when they talk about the inconsistency, incompetence, and outright idiocy of the child welfare system, and many of the people who work in it. But people don't go into that line of work because it's easy money. They do it because they want to help people. The best of them establish personal relationships with the children they are assigned to work with. But they can't love them as a grandparent can; there are simply too many. And the system that they serve, by its very nature, cannot love even one child, no matter how forcefully it insists that its purpose is to serve their best interests.

FIFTEEN

Caseworkers' Conflicting Priorities: Closing Files vs. Helping Children

*Government is filled with good
people trapped in bad systems.*

—Al Gore

WANTED: CASEWORKER

*Goes into homes where child abuse and neglect are
suspected and makes objective assessments. Apprehends
children from unsafe homes and acts professionally
when a judge sends them back. Empathetic, creative
problem-solver, emotionally detached from clientele and
immune to trauma. Coaches addicted mothers and fathers in how to parent. Must not expect results or positive
feedback. Skilled at shielding the minister so he/she isn't
embarrassed on the evening news. Acts in the best interest of the child, closes files, and saves government money.*

—*A hypothetical Children's Services job posting*

By the time he left, in 2004, Jim Mullins had worked for Alberta Children's Services for nineteen years. He told me he was good at keeping the sad situations he dealt with every day from traumatizing him, but he had trouble coping with a toxic work environment that was "punitive toward staff" and in which "there was always pressure to spend less."

"I had a young fellow who lived with his grandmother," he told me. Jim was the PGO[1] worker at the time, and his mandate was to find permanent, stable homes for children. His supervisor and others in the system pressured him to ask the grandmother when she was going to adopt the boy. The grandmother was comfortable with the government support she was getting, he said, and was not ready to give that up. Despite his own discomfort, he asked her several times if she wanted to adopt her grandson, and she'd say she was thinking about it. "I found it frustrating," he said. "It was clear to me, if she wanted to adopt him, she would approach me. Every so often I was to ask her…because then he'd be another kid off the caseload. I thought it was unethical to put pressure on a family member to do that.…My view of adoption," Jim continued, "is if it's going to work, everybody has to be willing, as opposed to feeling they're being pushed."

The department usually served clients well, he said, but its fiscal priorities got in the way. Clients in therapy would

---

1 Permanent Guardianship Order. When a judge issues a PGO, the province becomes the child's legal guardian. A foster home, group home, or family member is simply the caregiver.

be cut off "purely for financial reasons." He told me that every January, February, and March, "you could anticipate that people would be cut off just because it was the end of the fiscal year and money was running out." Politicians have to manage the public treasury, but Children's Services isn't a business. It's there to protect traumatized and vulnerable children when their parents can't or won't.

The constant financial squeeze and the mandate to shelter the minister from negative publicity created a culture that depersonalized caseworkers. Jim left because he didn't feel valued or supported. He told me of a 10-year-old girl on his caseload with a history of heart disease. "She and her siblings were in foster care. One day in school, she basically collapses. She was running for the school bus. So they rush her to the hospital. I get word and go to the Royal Alex." Jim looks out my west-facing window and points toward the Royal Alexandra Hospital, less than a kilometre away. "I was there in the emergency when they declared her dead." His throat tightened. He paused to take a deep breath. "The next day, there was pressure on me to produce this document so the minister or somebody could respond to the anticipated media inquiries," he said. "This girl was on my caseload and she died! I was at the hospital when she died! There was no concern for me. The concern was to feed the system some information." Furthermore, the corporate culture in the department, he said, was, "If the kid was on my caseload, it was my fault."

After nineteen years of uncaring supervisors, fear of being blamed when something went wrong, and feeling unvalued, Jim had to leave the work he loved. He said that during the latter part of his tenure, he "made the decision that my employer was only going to get from me what they paid for." He became a "nine-to-fiver" to protect himself from further abuse by the system, which meant that service to his clients suffered. "I had my own standard that I felt I was not always meeting," he said. "And I didn't feel good about that."

Jim was born in Leicester, England, in the late 1940s. He was the oldest of six siblings, so he took on a caregiving role while he was growing up. His first job was in computer programming, but the intellectual satisfaction he got in the late '60s, "with this bloody computer the size of a house," wasn't enough. He wanted to work with people, so he went into social work.

When he got his social work degree in 1975, the world was much different than it is now; it was the same world I and many skipped-generation grandparents grew up in too. He first worked with young offenders. The most common offenses were joyriding, break and enters, glue sniffing, shoplifting—mainly property-type crimes like breaking into a home, emptying the freezer, and just throwing frozen meat on the floor. Some kids were charged with marijuana or alcohol possession. Jim couldn't remember any "aggressive behaviours." These days, he said, kids in junior high are caught dealing drugs in school hallways. His most recent work was with teenage sex offenders. "My sense is that even back in the seventies, this was happening," he says. "It's just that nobody was talking about it. Not only that: I think the whole system wasn't geared to take a look at it, even to ask the right questions." In those days, he didn't know what signals to look for. He said he and his colleagues would have done anything to avoid discussing sexual behaviour with teenagers, but now, "I can easily have those discussions, because that's part of my world."

His first exposure to Kinship Care was in the late '90s, when it was called Kindred Care. The financial support for caregivers was minimal, he said. "Compared to foster care, it was night and day," even more difference than now. He wished Children's Services could be more like it was in Edmonton in the '70s, when every city office was in the same building. He worked with young offenders, the public health department was in the basement, and they did home visits and programming together. He's convinced that if Children's Services developed more connections with community agencies and increased its joint programming, they could do more with less money. But he's noticed that, in Edmonton at least, the drive to save government money means Children's Services hires caseworkers with less education and experience, which makes it less likely they'll develop connections like that.

I interviewed one of those new caseworkers, a 26-year-old woman named Susan whose youthful exuberance, compassion, and idealism I hoped would compensate for her less impressive credentials. At the time, she had been on the job only three years. She had a caseload of twenty-nine children. The majority lived with their birth parents, and she coached and supported these parents to keep their families together. Like Jim, she said that Children's Services could serve everyone better by collaborating more with community groups and agencies.

"One of the most difficult aspects of my job is there really aren't the resources in the community to prevent or lessen their children's involvement with us," Susan said. What frustrated her was that the research on prevention is so clear: "If you put money into prevention and community services, you end up saving so much money with the criminal justice system and the family law system and Children's Services."

The cost of apprehending a child, going to court, paying lawyers and court workers, the ongoing cost of foster care, she said, are all much higher than "to have a child at home with their parents and paying a family support worker to go there twice a week and paying for other support." Not only is it cheaper, she said, but "it's way better for the child." And yet, "there's always pressure to close the file," she told me.

Her office is good at extending "family enhancement agreements" to support keeping families together, she said, but government policy doesn't put a high enough priority on "preventing drug and alcohol abuse, helping kids stay in school longer, preventing involvement in criminal activities and gangs."

Susan had two children in her caseload, siblings being raised by grandparents, and they require less time and energy than anybody else. That's because they are healthy and in a healthy relationship. In fact, she said, she looks forward to visiting this family every month because the calm, relaxed environment in the home feels almost like a vacation compared to what she faces with other families.

For example, she told me of families for whom she has court supervision orders that say there are "reasonable and probable grounds that a child's safety, security, and development will be protected in their parents' care," and the orders spell out conditions that must be met. An order could involve counseling for the parents at the Alberta Alcohol and Drug Abuse Commission, psychological assessments, parenting and addictions programs, et cetera. "They're definitely more time consuming for us," she said, "because we have to constantly assess risk and protective factors for the kids. If there's domestic violence, alcohol abuse, that sort of thing, I need to decide whether to go in and apprehend the kids or not." She said she's had situations where she apprehended the kids, had to return them to their families under a supervision order, and then had to reapprehend them.

"The thing I always tell myself is, it's about the kids. The parents are adults, most of the time. If they want to abuse alcohol or drugs or be in a violent relationship, I'm gonna do whatever I can to get them the help they need, but I can't make them do anything." She paused and said, "Nobody can make anybody do anything. But I do have the power to take a child out of an unsafe situation. That's all I can do. It's definitely not easy."

The legislation Susan works under, the Child, Youth and Family Enhancement Act, defines a number of criteria that must be met to decide if a child is at risk, but it also includes what they call "matters to be considered," which says that "the family is the basic unit of society and its well-being should be supported and preserved."[2] "That's something I always try to remember," Susan said. "No matter how unhealthy a family is, it's still a family, and you love them no matter what. It doesn't mean a child should remain in that home, but it's also incredibly traumatic for a child to be apprehended and placed with complete strangers."

Most grandparents I've talked to would have a hard time putting "love" and "social worker" in the same sentence, but there it is. Social workers like Susan and Jim certainly don't do this kind of work for the money or because of any thanks they get.

Susan said that sometimes a social worker might make an informal arrangement with the extended family to avoid having the kids taken away. "I have a situation where the mom has three children who've been in care for three years," she explained. The family had a lot of involvement with Children's Services over the years. "Grandma was in residential school, mom is like ten days younger than me, and she's due with baby number four right away." The mom admitted to using crack cocaine during pregnancy. "She and her new boyfriend came into my office. We talked about two family members who I'm gonna connect with about being placements when the baby is born, and we looked at signing a custody agreement so

---

2   Section 2(a) of the *Child, Youth and Family Enhancement Act*, Revised Statutes of Alberta 2000, Chapter C-12.

mom and dad can go into treatment. That will prevent an apprehension order. It's a lot nicer for everyone when we can plan ahead like that. It keeps the baby safe, and mom and dad can do what they need to do. If they don't follow through, we'll have to deal with that then. But at least we can plan beforehand. It's never easy."

Not only is it not easy, but statistics show that addicts who go into rehab relapse between 40 and 60 per cent of the time.[3] And yet, despite the odds against rehab, and the traumatic scenes she encounters in family homes, Susan hasn't lost the youthful idealism she started with. When I asked her how she does it, she said, "It's totally the little stuff. It's too easy to feel you're not doing anything helpful." She told of a teenage boy who kept running away from his foster home. She'd been working with him for nine months when he called her from school one day. She went to meet with him, found out he was staying with a friend, and asked him where that was. When he told her, she was pleasantly surprised. "Most kids, when they're AWOL," Susan said, "wouldn't even talk to you or show up for school; there's no way they'd give me their friend's name and their friend's mom's name." She admits that this was a small thing, but it said that he trusted her, which meant she'd built a real relationship with him. And relationships are the key, she said.

She also told of a girl in grade 2, part of a "huge extended family," many of whom are involved in "drug

---

3   See http://luxury.rehabs.com/cocaine-addiction/recovery-statistics/.

trafficking, prostitution, that sort of thing." Most of them hated the police because they'd been picked up so often and had police in their homes confronting them. It was Halloween, and the girl had a costume on. Susan asked her what she wanted to be when she grew up. "She said 'I want to be a police officer, because I want to see people safe.' I wanted to cry," Susan said. "You know, some police officer has made a huge impact on her life."

They say imitation is the sincerest form of flattery, but "flattery" is the wrong word here. This grade 2 girl wanted to be a police officer for the same reason Susan became a social worker: someone helped her when she was in trouble. When Susan was in high school, her family informally adopted a boy from a horribly dysfunctional family. Susan's mother became the boy's Kinship Care mother. While Susan was partying, using drugs and alcohol with that boy's brother, the boy was himself learning to live a better life. As an adult, he now leads sports programs to help others like him. When Susan eventually entered rehab, several social workers and her own mother supported her and inspired her to become like them.

As inhuman and bureaucratic as the child welfare system can be, it's a system we've set up to backstop the parents, the extended family, the village that raises our children. People like Susan and Jim, when they extend themselves beyond the boundaries of their job descriptions, are as good as the best brothers, sisters, cousins, aunts, uncles, and grandparents a child could have, even though it's only for a short time. By daring to love the work they do and the children they care for, they can inspire the next generation to imitate them.

The child welfare system reminds me of one of the most prophetic elements of *Star Trek: The Next Generation*: the Borg collective. The Borg collective consisted of half-human/half-machine beings whose objective was to assimilate everyone on the *Enterprise*, on Earth, and throughout the universe. At the end of season 3, when the Borg captures Captain Picard, he becomes part machine and struggles to maintain his humanity. The Borg keep repeating its mantra to the *Enterprise's* crew: "Resistance is futile. You will be assimilated."

Jim and Susan are proof that resistance is not only possible but necessary. Grandparents, too, are on the front line in the battle to safeguard the future of the human race. There is even evidence to show that grandparents' love and wisdom has been the key to human survival from the early days of our species.

SIXTEEN

Grandparents and the Survival of the Species

Grandparents are mutant superheroes.
—*Bob McDonald,* Quirks and Quarks, *CBC Radio.*

When it comes to grandmothering, humans have more in common with whales than with chimpanzees or apes. Forget relative brain size, opposable thumbs, use of tools, or the ability to walk upright; of the millions of animal species on the planet, only three have evolved to grandmother: killer whales, short-finned pilot whales, and humans. Only *Orcinus orca, Globicephala macrorhynchus,* and *Homo sapiens* live long enough after their reproductive years are over to be of use to their grandchildren.[1] The grandmother

---

1   See Lauren J. N. Brent, Daniel W. Franks, Emma A. Foster, Kenneth C. Balcomb, Michael A. Cant, and Darren P. Croft, "Ecological Knowledge, Leadership, and the Evolution of Menopause in Killer Whales," *Current Biology* 25, no. 6 (2015): 746–50.

hypothesis says that for all other species, an individual female's value to the species ends when she can't produce babies anymore. The grandfathers? Scientists are still trying to figure out what we're good for.

One way to understand the grandmother hypothesis is to look at species at the opposite end of the grandmothering spectrum, the Pacific salmon. At spawning time, males and females exhaust themselves swimming back to where their lives started, hundreds or even thousands of kilometres upstream. They die almost immediately after they lay and fertilize their eggs. Their children are on their own after that. No parents to hunt up juicy worms for them and feed them in the comfort of their own nests, like robins. No flying or hunting lessons, like ducks or bears. No toilet training. No snuggling up to mommy's breast for a suck of warm milk. Salmon hatchlings start life in cold water, on their own. They have to find food and avoid getting eaten until they mature and come back "home" to spawn and die. For adult salmon, reproduction and death are two halves of the same action.

Orcas, short-finned pilot whales, and humans, on the other hand, can live long after reproduction. They are the only species to experience menopause and go on to grandmother. The grandmother hypothesis says menopause is an adaptive response that strengthens the gene pool and ensures the survival of the species. Grandmothers are not just nice older women who spoil grandchildren.

Female killer whales reproduce from age 12 to 40, but they can survive into their nineties. Males usually die by

50. No grandfathering for them! The research says male and female adults stay with their mothers, and so do the grandchildren. Older females are especially valuable to the family groups they lead when their preferred food, Chinook salmon, gets scarce. Their ability to remember where to find food in times of scarcity can be the difference between survival and starvation. The longer a female killer whale lives, the more valuable she is to the group, not only for finding food but to avoid predators, to strengthen social connections in the group, and to contribute to what scientists call "collective cognition."[2] Collective cognition is not groupthink or conformism; rather it refers to the shared memory and wisdom of elders among the group. Killer whales survive not because they use the same Twitter feeds or follow the same news broadcasts, but because they live in integrated social groups and value their (female) elders' shared wisdom.

When *Homo sapiens* began, about two hundred thousand years ago, the grandmothers' role in species survival would have been clearer than it is now there are over seven billion of us. People who live in caves and depend on nuts, berries, and wild animals for food must stick together to survive. They don't roam far from their families, and if they have to move because it's a bad year for picking berries or hunting boars, the whole extended family moves as a group. They stay in shelter that protects them from the elements, from large predators, and from rival families or tribes.

2   Brent et al., "Ecological Knowledge, Leadership, and the Evolution of Menopause in Killer Whales."

Hunter-gatherers didn't have the luxury of homes in the suburbs and air-conditioned cars to commute to and from work. They didn't have supermarket shelves stocked full of meat, fruit, and vegetables from all over the world every day of the year. They didn't have bank accounts, income tax, cancer clinics, or smart phones, and they couldn't fly around the world on jumbo jets. Like killer and pilot whales, they lived together in extended family groups and honoured their elders for the knowledge and wisdom they shared.

Whether ancient or modern, grandmothers who live near their adult children give child-care advice and provide child care themselves. They do it when the parents are working, socializing, or collaborating with neighbours, and when children are ill or newborn. Unfortunately, Western society today places little value on child care, whether it's provided by grandparents, parents, or day-care staff. Childcare is among the lowest-paid work, if it's paid at all. And, unlike what happens among Indigenous peoples, early humans, or killer whales, we also treat older people mostly as burdens, instead of valuing them as repositories of wisdom. That's changed somewhat in recent years with the aging of baby boomers like me who outnumber the generations before and after, who live longer and healthier lives, and who have economic and electoral muscle to flex. Even so, retired people are usually taken for granted. We're expected to do volunteer work because people think we don't have much to do and that our time isn't worth much anyway.

Because of workforce mobility and the fact that most of us live in cities, large numbers of young parents have to raise children without grandparents close by. My biological grandchildren now live 300 and 3,000 kilometres away. When I was growing up, I lived 3,000 kilometres from my grandparents. When my own children were little, we lived between 2,000 and 3,000 kilometres away from their grandparents. I was jealous whenever I met young parents my age whose parents would drop in and help with the kids on short notice, take the kids for a parents' weekend or vacation break, or manage the house when the parents took sick or had another baby. Like so many others in our mobile workforce, my wife and I were on our own.

Humans are supposed to be the most intelligent of species, the top of the food chain, the apogee of four billion years of evolution, the crowning glory of what some call the universe's "intelligent design." So why are we determined to destroy each other and the Earth and to make life more difficult for our children instead of helping our species survive? The same economic system that enables our mobility and separates us from extended families devalues child care. Some say we've overpopulated the planet and we're driving other species extinct at an alarming rate. They claim that the upside of war, climate change, and incurable diseases is that the Earth will be better off when we finally drive ourselves toward extinction. Some say if we just let women run the place, our species and our planet would have a brighter future.

But what about grandfathers then? Why isn't there a grandfather hypothesis? When my kids were growing up, I was away from home working much of the time. I spent as much time with them as I could, but it was a father's job to work and pay the bills. I commuted sixteen kilometres each way to work every day and worked forty hours and more every week. If I'd been an emperor penguin, I'd have formed a large circle on Antarctic ice with other males, held an egg on my feet, and gone two months without food—in the dark!—to protect it from -60 degree temperatures. I'd have stood to attention like a well-trained palace guard while my mate gorged herself in open water and returned months later with something in her gut to feed our newly hatched baby. But penguins don't live long enough to be grandfathers.

So why do we male humans live long enough to see our children have children? The grandmother hypothesis says that for killer whales, wisdom or "collective cognition" comes through grandmothers. The males simply die off when they can't reproduce anymore. Grandfathering just isn't for them. They don't live long enough to impart wisdom. They don't become pod leaders. They're as irrelevant to the species as the drone honeybee is after he's won the race to mate with the queen and deposited his genetic material in her body. The 50-year-old orca and the post-coital drone both die because they've fulfilled their purposes in life. They're simply done.

In a 2007 study to see if grandfathering could be the reason human males live as long as females, researchers concluded that grandfathering has probably had a negligible impact over the millennia of our evolutionary past.[3] They note that males can father children well beyond the age of menopause, and that this is the only evolutionary reason they can find for males to live long enough to be grandfathers: because they can still father children when they're old—providing they can find a young woman to mate with! They say nothing about wisdom or nurturing or playing with grandchildren. Nothing about cuddling up with grandma and supporting her in her role. Their conclusion may or may not be true. Maybe there simply aren't older men doing scientific research on the subject to put up a good argument for our side.

A study published at the end of 2015 added another wrinkle. It concluded that "humans have evolved gene variants that can help protect the elderly from dementia." The study's lead author, Dr. Ajit Varki of the UC San Diego School of Medicine, noted that "such genes likely evolved to preserve valuable and wise grandmothers and other elders."[4] The study included elders of all genders, and it didn't differentiate among them. But before we take Bob McDonald's "grandparents are mutant superheroes" quip too seriously, we should note what Dr.

---

3   M. Lahdenpera, A. F. Russell, and V. Lummaa "Selection for long lifespan in men: Benefits of grandfathering?" *Proceedings of the Royal Society B: Biological Sciences* 274 (2007), 2437–44.

4   See Flavio Schwarza, Stevan A. Springera, Tasha K. Altheidea, Nissi M. Varkia, Pascal Gagneuxa, and Ajit Varki, "Human-specific derived alleles of CD33 and other genes protect against postreproductive cognitive decline," Proceedings of the *National Academy of Sciences* 113, no. 1 (2016), 74–9.

Deborah Blacker, a genetic epidemiologist at Harvard University, said about the 2015 study: that until fifty years ago, very few people lived long enough to get late-stage Alzheimer's.[5] Fifty years is not nearly enough time for *Homo sapiens* to evolve or to gather reliable data to support a grandfather hypothesis.

Nonetheless, I'm happy to stand in the pantheon of mutant superheroes alongside Betty, Victoria, Ruth, Maria, Chris, Trina, Jim, Meghan, Mary, Greg, Cindy, Tom, April, Luke, Ann, Linda, Olive, Natalie, Tania, Derek, Marcel, all the others I've met, as well as the other many thousands of grandparents I haven't met. We should all give ourselves superhero names to honour what we do, names like Betty the Bear, Laughing Trina, Magical Marcel, Cool Hat Luke. I'll be Gary the Grey.

Whether science can prove it or not, all of us skipped-generation grandparents know we're doing vital work. Our species may not be at risk of extinction, but we are each doing our part to ensure the survival and success of our grandkids. My hope is that everyone who reads this book will understand how much skipped-generation grand-parents contribute to the health and future of our world, and that they'll do at least one thing to collaborate with these superheroes. Maybe listening to someone's story is enough. Maybe you can improve government policy or correct a flaw in the child welfare system. The chances are pretty good that you already know some grandparents

---

5   Angus Chen, "Grandkids Could Be One Reason Humans Live Long Lives," National Public Radio, December 1, 2015.

like us. I hope that since you've read this far, you know now that for those of us raising grandchildren, there really is nothing better for us to do. And you may someday become a *grand*parent yourself.

Some Grandparenting Resources

CANADA

Parent Support Services Society of BC
Grandparents Raising Grandchildren
Support Line: 1-855-474-9777
www.parentsupportbc.ca/
grandparents-raising-grandchildren

CANGRANDS National Kinship Support
Tel: 613-334-4246 Email: grandma@cangrands.com
www.cangrands.com

Creating Hope Society
("An Aboriginal home for every
Aboriginal child in care by 2025")
creatinghopesociety.ca

Canadian Child Welfare Research Portal
cwrp.ca/statistics

Ontario Health Promotion E-bulletin
www.ohpe.ca/node/6892

UNITED STATES

American Grandparents Association

aga.grandparents.com

Grandfamilies

www.grandfamilies.org

Child Welfare Information Gateway

www.childwelfare.gov

Grandparents as Parents

grandparentsasparents.org

UNITED KINGDOM AND AUSTRALIA

Grandparents Plus (UK)

www.grandparentsplus.org.uk

Grandparents Information: Supporting Queensland Grandparents (AU)

www.grandparentsqld.com.au

Gary Garrison is the author of *Human on the Inside: Unlocking the Truth about Canadian Prisons*, holds a PhD in English from the University of Alberta, and was editor of Alberta Hansard. He lives in Edmonton.